CRAFTY ITALIAN COOKERY

Michael Barry

D1556029

JARROLD PUBLISHING

MICHAEL BARRY'S CRAFTY ITALIAN COOKERY

JARROLD PUBLISHING
Whitefriars, Norwich

Designed and produced by
THE ERSKINE PRESS
Banham, Norwich

Recipes by Michael Barry
Food for photography by
The Banham Bakehouse, Norfolk
Food Styling by Lesley de Boos
Photographs © Andrew Perkins
Designed by jack afrika Associates

Printed in England

CONTENTS

INTRODUCTION

Italy is the most diverse and in many ways the most extraordinary of all the great countries of Europe. Geographically it extends from the highest peak of the Alps almost to North Africa, from the Alpine snows to the burning South. It's a country whose political and artistic heritage is at the heart of the West's history and culture. And yet, as a country it has only existed for one hundred and thirty years. As long ago as 500 BC there were two great confederations ruling Italy, the Greeks in the south, and in the north the Etruscan confederation. Both founded cities whose names ring down the ages and which can still be visited and enjoyed today: Bologna and Perugia, Rome, Naples and Palermo. Then for half a millennium the great Empire of Rome dominated the world west of China. After its fall, nearly a thousand years later, the intellectual blossoming of the Italian Renaissance, underpinned by massive trade and finance development, brought the great cities of Florence and Venice and Genoa into worldwide prominence. And all the time throughout this period the Popes of Rome and the religion they served spread outwards to become one of the most far-reaching of influences.

But Italy as a concept was more real than Italy as a country and it wasn't until the end of the nineteenth century, that the whole of the 'boot' of Italy and its 'football' Sicily became united as one nation. Since then it's had a turbulent time politically and militarily, siding with the Allies in the First World War and the Germans in the Second. But for the last fifty years it has emerged as one of the leading states in the new confederation of Europe. A nation of economic, cultural and stylistic power, the equal of any of its neighbours.

Despite its reputation for political chaos Italy runs itself remarkably well and remarkably calmly. There's a sense of ease in the Italian lifestyle, a desire to enjoy life and whatever it offers, and to enjoy doing as little as possible where possible: 'dolci fa niente', meaning the pleasure of doing nothing, is central to the attraction of the country. This is not to reinforce any of the stereotypes that southern Italians are lazy (a quick visit to Naples would correct any misconception like that) but that pleasure is regarded as highly as duty.

One of the greatest pleasures in Italy of course is the food, a fact the Italians recognise well by still allowing themselves two hours for lunch. Almost every bank and shop in every city will grind to a halt and only the restaurants will bustle between 12.30 and 2.30 pm, and it's a pleasure that the rest of the world has learned to come and share. Every major city in the world has its Italian restaurants. There is even a view that it was the Italians who taught the French to cook when a Florentine Medici princess took her cooks with her on marrying a French king. Whatever the truth of that, there's no question that there is a great tradition of feasting and of peasant fare throughout the country. These two traditions run both separately and intermingled

< 4 >

and, as is so often the case in the late twentieth century, it's the peasant food that's often the basis for the most fashionable cooking in even the most expensive restaurants these days.

Italian food reflects the extraordinary variety of the country. Whether it's the bean soups of Tuscany or the huge luscious steaks of its capital, Florence, the wafer-thin pizzas that are eaten in the streets of Naples at breakfast time, or the pungent Arabic influenced pasta sauces of Sicily, there are always regional variations and surprises. There are the famous fish stews, varied in every province and indeed in almost every fishing village or town around the incredibly long Italian coast, but in such a variety of flavours and ways, from tomatoes and peppers to chilli and vinegar. There are the game dishes of the high mountains, the cream and egg-rich cooking of the great Bolognese plain, the chocolates and pastry of Turin, and the lamb and chilli sauce of Apulia. A range of flavours, textures, ingredients and cooking techniques that never fails to amaze and delight.

Despite the fact that almost every restaurant in every town or village claims to sell pizza as well as its own standard menu, there is always a regional speciality. Whether it is the style of the pasta, the nature of the sauce, the kind of fruit used in the fruit salad, or the ice-cream, it will typify the region. The fifty-eight million Italians are spread right across the country. Even the largest city, Rome, with its three million, doesn't dominate the country in the same way that Paris or London dominate their nations. The result is that the regional centres retain a strong identity, they were, after all, mostly independent states only one hundred and fifty years ago, and their food styles reflect this. They reflect also the climate. In the north, up near the Alpine border, the snow may lie on the ground for five months of the year and warm weather 'Mediterranean' cuisine is neither appropriate nor very popular. In the deep south, below Naples, except for cheese, the milk products so central to the cooking of Bologna are hardly known, and the tomato and its close friend, garlic, reign supreme. Every region has its own kind of pasta. Pasta in every conceivable size and shape and colour, from dark red through pale white to burnished gold. Pasta two feet long and pasta less than the size of a grain of rice. Pasta for sauces, pasta for pies, pasta for soups and pasta for gratins. Commercially made, home made, dried and fresh, pasta is the great staple and joy of Italian cooking. In places even pasta has alternatives like rice or polenta, or the cornmeal porridge which once again is proving so popular and palatable around Venice and the centre of the Italian food industry in the Po Valley.

Eating out in Italy is always a pleasure and although the cuisine varies from region to region the pattern is usually similar if you are eating a full meal. You may find that more than one of these a day is more than the human frame can stand because they're certainly not lacking in substance or flavour. Properly undertaken they should begin with some *antipasti* which may include local vegetables, salamis, or even, in some regions, cheeses. There follows the pasta dish itself which, just to confuse, may actually be made of rice or semolina, as in the little dumplings called *gnocchi*, it may even include polenta. There will then follow a main course, meat or fish based and perhaps with a vegetable, though that may be served separately. Some

< 5 >

regions have a cheese course at this point, as they do in France, and some do not, preferring to eat the cheese with fruit. Puddings are more a restaurant speciality. Most restaurants and cafés will serve some form of tart, fruit salad and, without question, ice-cream, both the creamy kind and *granita*, made from crushed ice and fruit or coffee flavourings. The meal will always finish with a tiny cup of intensely strong expresso coffee, totally different to any that you've ever experienced in Britain, which acts in its own way as a digestive. Wine is drunk with the meal but not as devotedly as it might be in France, and water, particularly one of the many *aqua minerales*, which are as regional as the food, will almost certainly come into play. Lunch is still, in some places, the main meal, although, in cities, the habit of eating a substantial dinner after a lighter lunch has crept in, particularly amongst the business communities.

Italy abounds with great restaurants with ancient traditions and tiny trattoria or cafés tucked away around the corner of the most unexpected building or alleyway. Exploring cities or towns or even villages for these undiscovered gems is one of the great pleasures of travelling in Italy, and in each chapter in this book I have suggested the sort of food that you might look for in each of the regions.

The book itself is divided into twelve regions, slightly arbitrarily as in one or two cases I've grouped provinces together because of the similarity of their food and climate and agriculture. Sometimes they are regions that have anciently been joined, as in the Emilia-Romagna which has been regarded as a single province for more than 400 years. Some of the provinces, of course, are so big that they have quite varied characters and some are dominated by one or occasionally two great cities. In all cases I've tried to look for what makes the place unique and gives it its own special character. Each chapter has an introduction to the region with a little history and background as well as the main topic of food and cooking. There's a suggestion as to how to get the best out of eating out and then the recipes, ranging from *antipasti* to puddings in each case. I ought to emphasise that this is an arbitrary selection of recipes and a 'crafty' one at that. I've chosen recipes I particularly like. It's not meant to be a scholar's appraisal of the whole range, and in every case I've tried to choose recipes and construct ways of cooking them that can be achieved here in Britain. There are, of course, always ingredients and special materials that you can only find in the local area or region itself and, delicious though some of these are, there's no point in offering recipes for which you can't find the ingredients. I have tried to take as few liberties as possible but these are essentially crafty Italian recipes designed to be cooked in British kitchens, and so I ask forgiveness from any purists who feel that the shortcuts are not what their momma taught them.

I've been lucky enough to know and love Italy and its cuisine since I was a teenager. I've had many Italian friends, neighbours and restaurateurs and cooks. But in addition to my own experience I ought to offer some particular thanks to Valentina Harris and Antonio Carluccio, who I've watched and learned from in admiration for many years. In planning the book too, I was much inspired by Claudia Rodin's book on the food of Italy and Marcella Hazan's books on

< 6 >

Italian food. I'm also indebted to the hundreds of Italian cooks, restaurateurs, trattoria owners, waiters and ordinary citizens who have welcomed me and my appetite and enquiries, always with that grace and generosity of spirit that so typifies the very best of Italy.

Finally, no list of thanks for this book could be complete without a mention of the help and hospitality we received when taking the photographs, many of them shot in Italy, on location. There were farmhouses on Tuscan hillsides, fishing quays in Sicily, the sweep of the bay of Naples and much more. The highlight for us all, though, was the time spent at the Casa Buitoni at Sansepulcro on the Tuscan/Umbrian border. A magnificent palazzo with hospitality and views to match, it is now the headquarters of the Buitoni pasta and food empire. There we had the chance to learn about new directions and old skills in Italian cooking, and not least to meet and enjoy the wonderful company of Marisa Conti, Pierluigi de Micheli and their colleagues. They epitomised the welcome we found all over their wonderful country, generous, knowledgeable and full of the joy of life. Mille grazie!

Casa Buitoni

< 7 >

< 8 >

LOMBARDY & THE MILANESE

In many ways Lombardy and its great capital city, Milan, is the heart of modern Italy. Even more than Rome, it is the industrial centre and the financial hub around which so much of Italy's commerce revolves. Geographically the region is very varied, stretching from the great lakes of Como and Maggiore and Lake Garda in the north, down to the basin of the Po river, the great Lombard plain famous for centuries for the growing of grain.

Despite the geographical variety Milan itself has always dominated the region, artistically, financially and militarily. It was in Milan that Leonardo Da Vinci painted, and Milan is home to La Scala, the most famous of all opera houses, where many of the great operas of Verdi and Puccinni were first heard. Today, Milan is also the fashion centre of Italy and one of the great centres of the world for clothes. It's the base of the Italian film industry, and it's here too that a lot of Italian publishing and broadcasting takes place. Milan is therefore in many ways like a capital rather than a regional city, and its food, although there are many dishes known as Milanese, has often been overwhelmed by other regional and national specialities. Fast food abounds and there is a wide range of pizza and pasta houses set up by the hundreds of thousands of southern Italians who came north to find their fortune and work. As a result it's often in the other cities and towns of the region that the more traditional foods of the area can be found.

After the great Italian Dukes of Milan, the area was governed by the Spanish for two hundred years from the middle of the sixteenth to the eighteenth century, when in turn the Austrians succeeded them. It was 'liberated' by Napoleon and subsequently became part of the united Italy. The cuisine of the region shows a few of these influences, with the Austrian taste for breaded escalopes and chops being reflected in the dishes described as Milanese. But the most interesting thing about the region is how the cities have maintained their individual styles and cuisines. The famous Mostarda di Cremona, a chutney made of whole small fruits cooked in a sweet and sour syrup heavily flavoured with mustard oil, is eaten with boiled meats and salamis of all sorts. It's also used occasionally as part of the filling for various stuffed pastas, which are unique to the region. Near Piacenza there is a tradition of making sauces with nettles, and in the mountains the tradition is for small birds, quail and other similar species, to be grilled on long skewers and served on polenta.

< 9 >

It is an incredibly rich agricultural land with vast crops of grain creating staples both of wheat, as in pasta, maize and polenta, and rice, which is universally consumed. This last was, until recent years, regarded as rich man's food, but the passion for risottos produces an endless range of variations as well as the classic saffron coloured Risotto a la Milanese. The wealth of vegetables is traditionally shown in the wide variety of *minestra*, the generic name for minestrone soups which are eaten throughout the region, hot and cold! Veal is widely eaten, chicken enjoyed, beef has become a regular part of the diet, and rabbit is a great delicacy, eaten almost as often as chicken. The area is also famous for its cheeses. Perhaps the best known internationally is gorgonzola, which comes in both a plains and mountain variety. Bel paese comes from the region, and the Lombardy version of grana is made into padano, like parmesan, as a cheese for grating and cooking as well as eating fresh. In recent years perhaps the most famous cheese is mascarpone, made by curdling milk with citrus acids. It produces a creamy, almost sweet, cheese that is used widely in puddings and pastries. It's the basis for Tiramisu, a famous modern Italian pudding made originally in the Veneto, but eaten in lots of versions in and around Lombardy as well. In fact Lombardy is one of the few parts of Italy where puddings are frequently found. They're usually fruit based, whether fig mousses, or apricots or peaches baked with almond stuffing. There's also a strong tradition of cooking with pancakes, which may have been brought by the Austrians. Last but not least, Lombardy is one of the few parts of Italy where chocolate is used significantly in cooking, particularly to make a range of mousses and torones, or chocolate gateaux, that are eaten as a succulent ending to what is often an already filling cuisine.

Milan cathedral

< 10 >

EATING OUT

As Milan is, without question, the most cosmopolitan city in Italy, it's here that you can eat all kinds of regional variations that are not necessarily from Milan or Lombardy at all. In fact it's often quite difficult to find Lombard style cooking, or even the traditional Milanese forms. So many people have come from other parts of Italy to find work in Milan and have brought with them their own styles and traditions that these have become adopted and adapted. There are some very grand but pricey restaurants in Milan, particularly in and around the great Galeria, arguably the first shopping mall in the world, which leads off the Piazza del Duomo, the cathedral square at the centre of Milan. The Cathedral itself is an extraordinary 'hedgehog of a building' with literally hundreds of spires overlooking its square and lined with stylish and extremely pricey cafés – with highly coloured tablecloths, to identify them. Many of the smaller restaurants through the city serve food from the other regions of Italy – often to an outstanding standard.

Food shops are another great speciality of the city. What is often regarded as the greatest food shop in Europe, Peck, is here, but in addition there are many other shops in the area around it selling fresh and gourmet specialities. In the city itself it's worth looking for some of the latteria, literally milk bars, many of which have recently become quite inexpensive cafés serving a small but well made menu.

Further afield there's a much more regionally based cuisine. Up near the lakes in the Alpine foothills the food tends to have a stronger Austrian flavour. There is some lake fish, though that's getting very scarce these days and is often quite expensive. The restaurants with verandas actually looking over the lake tend to charge according to the view as much as for the cooking, but there are often very pleasant places to be found in the backstreets. While each of the towns has its own reputation, it's Cremona and Mantua which have substantial and separate cooking traditions. As well as its famous mostarda preserves, Cremona specializes in a number of soups, often based on pumpkin and sometimes flavoured with barley. Mantua, on the edge of the great Venetian plain, is well known for its dishes based on polenta, that great cornmeal porridge, a speciality of Venice itself. But it retains, even then, its own individuality, with a range of grilled meats and sausages to be eaten with the polenta, that is all its own.

In Lombardy it's worth remembering that Italy has a winter, and very often the dishes of autumn and the cold months are as rewarding and interesting as those of the summer. Particularly up in the hills towards the Alps rich casseroles and stews are widely prepared, such as the famous Osso Bucco, featuring slow simmered leg of veal with various flavourings. The slow simmering is the characteristic of these cold weather mountain dishes, and it's without question one of the treats of touring or winter sporting in the region in autumn and winter to have the pleasure of enjoying some of the richest and most robust food in the whole of Italy.

< 11 >

The Galeria, Milan

< 12 >

MINESTRONE SOUP

We tend to think of Minestrone as a tomato based vegetable and pasta soup. Not so – it is a rich broth and although it does contain vegetables it uses only those in season. The only real essentials are the dried white or pale green beans and some pasta or rice. The vegetables may be the leeks, carrots and cabbage of autumn and winter; broad beans, mushrooms and cauliflower in the spring; or pumpkin, tomatoes, courgettes and peppers in high summer. Here is a winter version and a summer one too.

Serves 4–6 as a starter

WINTER MINESTRONE

Ingredients

225 g/8 oz dried cannellini or haricot beans (or a 450 g/1 lb tin)
225 g/8 oz each celery, carrots and turnips, chopped

1.2 litres/2 pints beef stock   2 tbsp olive oil
50 g/2 oz small pasta shapes   2 onions, chopped
225 g/8 oz mushrooms, chopped   100 g/4 oz green cabbage shredded

Salt and freshly ground black pepper
Good pinch each dried oregano, thyme and basil
Freshly grated parmesan and crusty bread, to serve

Method

Soak the dried beans overnight. Drain and add to the stock in a large pan. Boil fast for at least 20 minutes, then simmer for about 2 hours, or open the tin and drain well. Heat the oil in a frying pan and sauté the onions, celery, carrots and turnips for 3–4 minutes until softened. Add these and the pasta and herbs to the beans. Season well and simmer for 15–20 minutes until the pasta is tender. You may need to add a little more water at this point. Add the mushrooms and cabbage and simmer for 5 minutes. Ladle into warmed soup bowls and serve sprinkled with the parmesan.

< 13 >

SUMMER MINESTRONE

Ingredients

225 g/8 oz dried cannellini or haricot beans (or a 450 g/1 lb tin)
1.2 litres/2 pints chicken stock or water

2 tbsp olive oil   **2 chopped onions**

225 g/8 oz each ripe tomatoes, courgettes and green peppers

175 g/6 oz peas (frozen are okay)   **50 g/2 oz rice**

50 g/2 oz chopped parsley   **Salt and pepper**

Freshly grated parmesan cheese and crusty bread, to serve

Method

Soak the dried beans overnight. Drain and add to the stock in a large pan. Boil fast for at least 20 minutes, then simmer for about 2 hours, or open the tin and drain well. Heat the oil in a frying pan and sauté the peeled and finely chopped onion, the peppers, split, seeded and cut into 5 mm/¼ in strips, and the courgettes, cut into 5 mm/¼ in rounds. Cook for 3–4 minutes. Add the vegetables and the rice to the beans and stock and simmer for 10 minutes. Cut the tomatoes into quarters, add those and the peas (if you're using fresh peas add those with the courgettes) and simmer for another 5 minutes or so. Stir in the chopped parsley and serve with parmesan and bread.

ZUPPA PAVASE

Legend has it that this soup is a modification of minestrone that a peasant woman made for the French king, Francois I, making it posh by adding expensive ingredients like eggs and cheese. However, modern Zuppa Pavase has none of the vegetables of a traditional minestrone. Coming from the town of Pavia it's quite a delicate soup made with a whole egg poached in consommé. It can be made with chicken or beef consommé and indeed is delicious with a simple strained chicken stock. I have used tins of consommé to make this dish, but it seems to leave a slightly processed food flavour in such a delicate process.

Serves 4.

< 14 >

Ingredients

4 slices white bread   50 g/2 oz butter
4 eggs   100 g/4 oz freshly grated parmesan or padano
1.2 litres/2 pints boiling chicken stock or beef consommé

Method

Trim the four slices of bread of their crusts and fry them in butter until pale gold on both sides. Place each one in a soup bowl that will contain it flat. Old fashioned soup plates are best for this. Very carefully break an egg for each plate. I find putting the egg into a cup first and then pouring it carefully onto the fried bread is the best method. Sprinkle each raw egg with parmesan cheese and a little salt and pepper. Pour carefully into each soup plate approximately 300 ml/half a pint of the boiling stock. Don't pour it directly onto the egg, or it will break up. The idea is that the egg cooks in the hot stock, which is why it has to be boiling. Serve immediately. The white should have set and the yolk still be soft inside, to be stirred into the soup. A sprinkling of parsley on top I think improves the appearance and flavour.

PASTA PRIMAVERA

A simple vegetable pasta dish, with lots of spring colour and flavour. This is a slightly low fat version, but no less delicious for all that.

Serves 4.

Ingredients

225 g/8 oz pasta spirals – fusilli
225 g/8 oz each broccoli florets, young courgettes and
shelled peas or string beans
125 ml/5 fl oz fromage frais
Salt and freshly ground black pepper
30 g/1 oz butter
4 tbsp freshly grated parmesan

< 15 >

Gorgonzola alla creme p. 17; pasta primavera p. 15

< 16 >

Method

Start by cooking the pasta. Put a large saucepan of water on to boil and add a pinch of salt and a little olive oil. When boiling, put the pasta in and leave to boil for three minutes. Take it off the heat, put the lid on and leave it for 7 minutes. At the end of that time it will be perfectly cooked, not sticky but perfectly *al dente.* Meanwhile, put 1 cm/½ inch of water into a frying pan with a lid and bring to the boil. Cut the broccoli into small florets, shell the peas or trim the beans and trim the ends off the courgettes. Cut these lengthwise into four, then slice into batons about 5 cm/2 inches long. When the water is boiling, add the butter and put in the broccoli and the peas or beans, put the lid on, turn the heat up to maximum and cook for 5 minutes. Take the lid off, add a pinch of salt and the courgettes, put the lid back on and cook for another 2–3 minutes. The vegetables will be crisp and bright green. The pasta by this time should just be at the end of its 7 minutes. Drain the vegetables and the pasta and, in a big bowl, mix them together. Season generously, add the fromage frais and toss gently. (If you really don't care, you can use 4 or 5 tablespoons of double cream instead!) It is wonderfully creamy and succulent, green and gold. Sprinkle freshly grated parmesan over each serving and eat!

GORGONZOLA ALLA CREME

This is a rich but very simple sauce to make – perfect for the flat green noodles called 'tagliatelle verdi', which get their colouring from spinach. The sauce is made from the famous 'blued' cheese of the region – which melts to a wonderful creamy consistency.

Serves 4.

Ingredients

225 g/8 oz gorgonzola cheese
350 g/12 oz tagliatelle verdi
Grated rind of 1 lemon

50 g /2 oz butter
75 ml/3 fl oz double cream
1 tbsp chopped fresh parsley

Salt and freshly ground black pepper

< 17 >

Method

Remove any hard rind from the gorgonzola, then cream together with the butter. Shape into a roll using a piece of plastic film and chill in the fridge. Cook the pasta in a large pan of boiling salted water for 3 minutes. Take off the heat and set aside with the lid on for 7–8 minutes until just tender and cooked through. Slice the roll into 1 cm/½ in sections. Heat the cream gently in a pan but don't allow it to boil. Add the cheese and butter sections and stir over a low heat until melted. When the sauce is smooth, but not boiling, drain the pasta and stir in the sauce, lemon rind and parsley. Season with plenty of pepper and serve at once in wide-rimmed bowls.

CHICKEN SALAD AL GONZAGA

There is a tradition in the towns of Lombardy to go back to the recipe books of the courts that adorned and oppressed the cities in medieval and Renaissance times. Many of these books and manuscripts are now published in facsimile. This dish is inspired by just such a manuscript from Mantua and the Court of the Gonzagas. It makes use of the very rich dark vinegar produced in the neighbouring city of Modena, which has recently become as fashionable as balsamic vinegar. It has an ancient rich flavour that makes it seem like a meal in its own right.

Ingredients

2 little gem cos lettuces
375 g/12 oz cooked chicken breast (poached is best, roast okay)

30 g/1 oz mixed peel (as used in cakes)	1 lemon
30 g/1 oz sultanas	1 tbsp balsamic vinegar
½ tsp each salt, pepper and sugar	100 ml/4 fl oz olive oil

Method

Wash and break the cos lettuce into small, half-postcard size pieces and use to line 4 shallow bowls. Skin the chicken, remove any bones, and slice across the grain into 5 mm/¼ in strips. Arrange it on the lettuce and sprinkle with the sultanas and candied peel. Stir the salt, sugar and pepper into the vinegar until dissolved. Whisk with the olive oil and pour over the chicken and lettuce. This should be consumed within 10 minutes of dressing the salad, otherwise the lettuce will start to go limp.

< 18 >

RISOTTO ALLA MILANESE

The Italians cook risotto like no one else. If you use the right rice – arborio – this is an ambrosial dish! The rice should be slightly moist, almost creamy, and each grain should be separate with still just a little bite in it. Buy a piece of parmesan cheese, if you can, and grate it yourself. The difference is well worth it.

Serves 4–6.

Ingredients

1.2 litres/2 pints beef stock
75 g/3 oz butter
350 g/12 oz arborio (risotto) rice

Good pinch of saffron strands
1 small onion, chopped
100 g/4 oz parmesan or padano cheese, grated
Fresh green salad to serve

Method

Pour the stock into a pan and bring to the boil, then reduce to a simmer. Steep the saffron in two tablespoons of the warmed stock for 5 minutes or so. Heat half the butter in a heavy-based large frying pan and fry the onion until softened. Stir in the saffron mixture and rice with a wooden spoon until all the grains are coated. Add the rest of the stock, a ladleful at a time, waiting until each ladleful has been absorbed by the rice before adding the next one, stirring constantly. When all the stock has been absorbed and the rice is translucent, remove from the heat. Stir in the remaining butter and the parmesan and leave to stand for 2–3 minutes to allow the flavours to develop. This is the classic addition to Osso Bucco (below). It also goes wonderfully well with fresh asparagus, often served in Milan with a butter-fried egg on top. This makes for quite a substantial dish in its own right.

< 19 >

Risotto alla Milanese p. 19; osso bucco p. 21

< 20 >

OSSO BUCCO

This is the great and perhaps the most famous of all stews from Lombardy. It's made with the veal shin, not always an easily obtainable ingredient in the UK, and for some, veal is also a concern with regard to the way it's raised. This should no longer be a cause for concern if humanely raised British veal is used. I have made it regularly with oxtail in the past, but after the various scares about beef, oxtail has also become extremely difficult to find. It can be made with shin of beef or with shank of lamb. However, if you ask your butcher you should be able to get British veal shin, not an expensive cut and one which provides a combination of succulence and flavour which really makes this dish worth cooking.

Serves 4.

Ingredients

900 g/2 lb veal shin, cut into 4 cm/1½ in pieces across the bone
100 g/4 oz each of carrots, celery and onion, cleaned and chopped into
5 mm/¼ in dice

2 tbsp seasoned flour	**1 tin Italian tomatoes in juice**
100 g/4 oz butter	**2 tbsp parsley**
1 clove of garlic	**Grated rind of 1 lemon**

½ tsp each of dried or freeze-dried sage and oregano
150 ml/¼ pint water (white wine is also sometimes used)

Method

In a pan into which the veal slices (or your alternatives) will fit in one layer, sauté the carrot, onion and celery dice gently in the butter. Flour the veal slices and add them, cooking until golden on both sides. Season generously. Add the herbs and the tomatoes. Add enough water just to come level with the veal. Cover the dish and simmer gently on the top of the stove or in a moderate oven 325°F/170°C/160°C Fan/Gas Mark 3/simmering oven of the Aga for 1–1½ hours until the meat is so well cooked that it is almost falling off the bone. Peel and finely chop the garlic, add it to the grated lemon rind and the chopped parsley and mix together. Serve the veal with a generous spoonful of the vegetable sauce over each slice, and sprinkle with the gremolata as the garlic, parsley and lemon seasoning is known. This is normally and traditionally served with Risotto alla Milanese.

< 21 >

SEA BREAM WITH GREMOLATA

Sea bream is one of those fish that seems to have gone unnoticed in this country, though this is not the case in Italy. It's particularly good and widely available in fishmongers now. It's a round not a flat fish with solid flesh and a good flavour, but if you can't find it, any firm fleshed fish like haddock, halibut or monkfish will act as a good alternative. Gremolata is an Italian seasoning mixture that's normally used in the area around Milan to season veal dishes, such as Osso Bucco, but as it's a mixture of garlic, lemon and parsley, it happens to suit fish well, although it has a vigorous flavour and needs substantial fish to cope.

Serves 4.

Ingredients

2 tbsp olive oil
4 x 175 g/6 oz sea bream fillets (or firm white fish)
Juice and grated rind of 1 lemon
2 tbsp chopped fresh parsley,
2 garlic cloves, finely, chopped
30 g/1 oz butter
Salt and freshly ground pepper
Risotto or plain boiled rice, to serve

Method

Heat the olive oil in a large frying pan and gently fry the fillets for 3 minutes on each side. Season to taste and add the lemon juice. Turn the heat right down, cover and simmer for 3 minutes while you make the gremolata. Mix the parsley with the lemon rind and garlic. Place the fillets on individual warmed plates. Add the butter to the pan and allow to melt without browning, mixing with the cooking juices. Pour this over the fish fillets and sprinkle the gremolata mixture on top of each serving. Serve at once with the risotto or rice.

< 22 >

SCALLOPINI AL LIMONE

This is perhaps the simplest, and also perhaps the most delicious, of all the quick cooked dishes that use veal escalopes (the thin slices from across the leg). It's equally delicious, though slightly different, made with the turkey fillet escalopes that are now very widely available in Britain. Whichever you use, the cooking method is almost identical as the meat needs to be cooked extremely quickly as it is by nature very dry and quite firm. The lemon flavouring is delicious, and produces an extremely light sauce. In parts of Lombardy the escalopes of veal are substituted not by turkey but by similarly sized pieces of calves' liver, which makes an equally delicious dish though of a substantially different flavour.

Serves 4.

Ingredients

450 g/1 lb veal or turkey escalopes, cut 5 mm/¼ in thick and approximately the size of half a postcard (they can be beaten a little flat)

4 tbsp oil (olive or sunflower will do)   **30 g/1 oz butter**

50 g/2 oz seasoned flour   **Salt and pepper**

Juice of 2 lemons

Method

Have all the ingredients ready in advance and the plates warm and your family or guests sat down – this is not a dish to keep waiting. Put the oil and the butter into a frying pan into which all the meat can go flat. Put the flour into a plastic bag and add the escalope slices. Shake and tip on to a plate from which you can put them quickly into the pan. As soon as the butter has finished foaming, add the meat rapidly, being careful not to catch your fingers in the hot oil. Cook it for about 45 seconds a side and then turn, using a fish slice. Continue to cook for another 45 seconds to a minute over maximum heat. Transfer to the plates. Pour the lemon juice into the pan and scrape up all the bits in the pan over a medium heat. Season the escalopes generously with salt and pepper and pour a spoonful or two of the sauce over each one. Serve immediately. Sautéd potatoes are traditional with this but it's nice without any starch at all, perhaps with just some quickly cooked courgettes or green beans.

< 23 >

LAMB CHOPS ALLA MILANESE

Lamb is not a meat much associated with northern Italy, but this dish is definitely worth mentioning. While hardly low-fat it does have that very Italian virtue of spreading a small amount of meat a long way. It's ideally suited to the thin, machine-cut chops on sale in many butchers at very low prices. The egg and breadcrumbing is very much a traditional Milanese technique used for everything from brains through veal escalopes to slices of cheese.

Serves 4.

Ingredients

450 g/1 lb lamb chops, thinly cut
175 g/6 oz fresh white breadcrumbs
1 egg
Grated rind ½ lemon (optional)
4 tbsp olive oil
1 tbsp softened butter
Salt and freshly ground black pepper
Sautéd potatoes and broccoli florets, to serve

Method

Beat the egg in a shallow bowl and dip in the chops one at a time. Put the breadcrumbs with plenty of seasoning and the grated lemon rind, if using, in a deep bowl. Place the egged chops in it and turn until well coated with the crumbs. Repeat until all the chops are coated. Heat the oil in a large frying pan and gently fry the chops in a single layer for 6 minutes on each side. Just before the end of cooking, drain the oil, add the butter and turn up the heat until the sizzling stops. Serve at once with sautéd potatoes and broccoli or another green vegetable.

< 24 >

CREMA DI MASCARPONE

Mascarpone is the almost sweet cream cheese produced in the alpine end of Lombardy, which has become one of the most popular ingredients in Italian dessert cookery in the last fifty years. This is a very simple way of using it, one of a number of ways in which a crema is made. It uses raw eggs and it's worth noting that, in Britain at least, this is still regarded with some suspicion by the Ministry of Agriculture because of the dangers of salmonella. I strongly recommend you find eggs from an impeccable source for this dish, as it's much too good to miss. I prefer my Crema di Mascarpone made simply with a flavouring of orange, but varieties of flavours and liqueurs are used, so if you feel like experimenting with chocolate or strega or rum it would not be out of place.

Serves 4.

Ingredients

225 g/8 oz Mascarpone

75 g/3 oz caster sugar

2 eggs, separated

Grated juice and rind of 1 orange

Method

Blend the egg yolks and sugar together until they are pale lemony coloured – an electric beater is often the best way of achieving this. Add the orange juice and rind and stir into the Mascarpone. Mix until smoothly blended. Beat the egg whites until they are stiff and fold them into the cheese mixture. Pile the resulting cream into individual wine glasses and chill for up to 2 hours in the fridge. A slice of candied orange or a little more grated orange peel sprinkled over the top is a nice decoration.

PEACHES BAKED IN HONEY AND LEMON

Baked peaches are a great Lombardy speciality. You can make this very well with tinned peaches (in their own juice). It's a lovely cold weather dish with the memory of summer. People have been known to replace the stone of the peach with an amaretti biscuit in each half before baking.

Serves 4.

< 25 >

Ingredients

4 peaches or 400 g/14 oz can peach halves in natural juice

2 cardamom pods

1 tbsp clear honey

50 ml/2 fl oz white grape juice

1 tbsp sugar

Juice and rind of 1 small lemon

Crème fraîche, to serve

Method

Pre-heat the oven to 400°F/200°C/180°C Fan/Gas Mark 6/middle of the Aga roasting oven. If using fresh peaches, place in a pan of boiling water and leave for 1 minute. Remove with a slotted spoon and drain on kitchen paper. Peel, cut in half and remove the stones. Arrange the peach halves in a large ovenproof dish. Lightly bruise the cardamom pods and scatter them around. To make the syrup, place the sugar, honey, lemon juice and rind in a small pan and add the grape juice. Bring to the boil and simmer for 1–2 minutes until the sugar has dissolved. Pour over the peach halves and bake for 20–25 minutes, basting occasionally. Serve at once with a bowl of crème fraîche or let the peaches cool in the syrup and serve at room temperature.

CHOCOLATE TORTA

Milan and Turin are the two great centres of chocolate cookery in Italy. This chocolate mousse is unusual in that it's baked. It produces a very rich and firm mousse.

Serves 4–6.

Ingredients

225 g/8 oz dark bitter chocolate (look for 70% cocoa solids)

100 g/4 oz unsalted butter

75 g/3 oz caster sugar

4 eggs, separated

65 g/2½ oz plain flour

< 26 >

Method

Break the chocolate up and put it and the butter in a non-stick saucepan over a very low heat. You may prefer to put them into a bowl and place that in turn in a pan of boiling water. In a separate bowl, beat the egg yolks with the sugar and the flour. When the chocolate and butter mixture is completely melted (do not let it boil!) mix them well together. Beat the egg whites until they are stiff and fold those in carefully. Butter a 20 cm/8 in soufflé dish (you may wish to dust this with a little flour as well), pour in the chocolate mixture and bake at a very low temperature, 275°F/140°C/130°C Fan/Gas Mark 1/bottom of the simmering oven of an Aga for approximately 45–50 minutes. Take out of the oven and allow to cool out of the fridge for at least 2 hours. Chill for another 2 hours before serving. It's easiest served direct from the dish with a spoon, rather like moulding a firm ice-cream. It's very rich and is nice served with thin lemon biscuits.

Chocolate Torta

< 27 >

Portici – Turin

< 28 >

PIEDMONT

Piedmont has a special place in the hearts of the Italian people. Geographically it's right up in the north west of the country, bordering both France and Switzerland, and for many centuries it was part of the Duchy of Savoy which in turn was part of the Kingdom of France, and yet it is in Piedmont that the birth of modern Italy began. It was Piedmont's King, Victor Emanuel, who became the first King of Italy, and Piedmont's capital, Turin, that for four years was the first capital of united Italy before Rome took over in 1865.

Although Piedmont is a true part of Italy, it doesn't really fit any of the stereotypes. It's a region where butter is more frequently used in cooking than olive oil, where in great areas of country the snow can lie on the ground for six months of the year (particularly in the high Alpine valleys and pastures above the Val d'Aosta), where the people are known for their lack of public expressiveness and the cuisine is almost tomato-less. Alba, in the south, is famous as a gourmet centre, particularly because of white truffles, of which it is the world's unique producer, and south of Alba again there is the unexpected rice growing region of Piedmont. It's also the largest producer of meat, particularly of beef and veal, and accordingly one of the largest producers of cheeses. Surprisingly not just cows milk cheeses as in fontina, the famous cheese from the north of the province, but also a whole range of goats cheeses as well. There is a local version of gorgonzola called murianengo, and an extraordinary range of 'mashed' cheeses known as brus. They are a mixture of different cheeses mashed up together, allowed to ferment and then often mixed with a variety of grappa or other strong alcohol to make a kind of powerful cheesy cream.

Turin itself and its cooking have always been much influenced by French traditions such as the tradition of fancy cake and pastry making and many of the wonderful cafés to be found in and around Turin's great squares specialize in these. They also specialize in various forms of chocolate, in particular the Giandujotti or hazelnut chocolates which are a great speciality of the city.

Rather than a great traditional central cuisine, the city is known for all kinds of culinary bits and pieces; perhaps the most amusing of these is Grissini – long, thin, almost spaghetti-like bread sticks. Properly made in Turin they are very different from the ones you may see on most restaurant tables in British trattoria. Some are up to a yard and a half long, some are short and fat and hand rolled. In their ultimate form all are known particularly for having an irregular rather

< 29 >

than a perfectly formed factory based shape to them. They're eaten with the *antipasti* that are such a part of the style of eating in the region. The pattern is known here as *assaggi* or tastings whereby, instead of two or three or even four dishes appearing as part of the *antipasti*, as many as ten or twelve may appear in tiny quantities including vegetable dishes and some of the local cured or smoked meats. In addition to the traditional ones made with pork there is a reputation in some parts of Piedmont for goose and even donkey salamis. Less extraordinary perhaps are the many liver patés, and venison from the Alpine forests which is smoked and cured. The pasta course will usually consist of some of the long square or oblong shaped pasta known in the region as *tajarin* or one of the famous risottos. The meat courses tend to be stews or boiled meats rather than the grilled meats of other regions. Especially with the cold winters that so much of Piedmont experiences, beef and game of all sorts, cooked slowly in wine or occasionally sweet and sour sauces, are very much part of domestic and restaurant cookery. Perhaps most famous is *Bollito Misto*, a mixed boiled meat dish where the range of inclusions can be very long indeed. It almost always includes a chicken, a piece of beef and a piece of veal, an ox tongue, various sausages or stuffed trotters, and a number of vegetables. In its full form it's probably best eaten in restaurants, but there are many 'cut down' versions served at home.

After the main course French influences really take over. The habit of eating cheese before the pudding is one that continues in the area. The cheeses are rather good and, unusually in Italy, are served on a large cheese board for people to help themselves. The puddings too reflect French taste. In restaurants the tradition of pastry making continues, and all kinds of exorbitant confections can be found, particularly those including the hazelnuts and walnuts of the region. Other puddings tend to be of the bavarois variety with eggs, cream and sometimes fruits and nuts being blended together to produce custards and cream puddings. Perhaps the most famous of these is *zabaglione*, made from egg yolks and Marsala wine whipped together.

Last but not least there is the matter of truffles. There are truffles from other parts of Italy, but the white truffles of Alba are the most famous. It's a unique production; nowhere else in the world seems to grow these particular extraordinary underground white fungi. They are incredibly expensive and normally eaten raw, grated over pasta, eggs and occasionally salads. There's a huge festival for them in the Autumn, coinciding with the mushroom and grape harvests, so the celebrations are long and extended. White truffles are only ever eaten fresh and they can be obtained in one or two specialist shops in Britain which import them in the season. To say that they're not cheap is an understatement but they are so pungent that a little goes a long way, and if you're interested in the great tastes of the world it's worth investing in a small truffle to try at least once.

< **30** >

EATING OUT

There are really two ways to eat out in Piedmont, one is in Turin, the other is outside it, and the difference is really that dramatic. Although Alba and Asti are quite substantial towns in their own right, Turin is the only real city. With its huge industrial complexes, considerable wealth and enormous energy the food in Turin really differs quite a lot from that which you'll find in the small trattoria and inns and restaurants of the villages and towns in the rest of the province. That goes, of course, doubly for those up in the great Alpine valley of Aosta where the cooking and style is much conditioned by the altitude and the proximity to Switzerland. Cheese dishes, particularly the famous Fonduta, is really best eaten here, a replication in a way of the Swiss style fondue sauce, this time made with fontina cheese and, rather than eaten with bread chunks, poured over rice or occasionally pasta or polenta. It's here too that a lot of the best game dishes are to be found, including chamois venison in the season.

In Turin itself are some of the most famous restaurants in the whole of Italy, many of them specializing in dishes of the region, and most of them, it must be said, quite expensive. However slightly less formal dining has its rewards in Turin, particularly in the elegant colonnaded avenues and squares of the centre. The cafés of the city are legendary and specialize often in different kinds of pastries or brioches, very much in the French style. There is also a famous drink, Bicerin, which is a mixture of coffee, chocolate and hot milk. It's traditionally drunk at breakfast time but is a good pick-me-up or refresher at any time, particularly on a brisk autumn day. The cafés also serve vermouth, which was invented in Turin, and a range of the wines for which the region is famous.

The things to eat in both bars and restaurants are the sort of dishes that really require especially local ingredients or substantial skill. In the great restaurants try the Bollito Misto or the Fritto Misto, a less substantial but no less fattening mixture of foods which in this area often includes a surprising number of sweet ingredients as well as the more traditional liver, kidneys, chops, mushrooms, aubergines, courgettes, artichoke hearts, cauliflower and so forth. There is a particular sweet custard, allowed to set and then egg and breadcrumbed with apples and amaretti almond biscuits that should be tried in the Piedmontese version of this dish. Do make sure that you get your share of the *assaggi*. It's worth asking the restaurateur if they indulge in this very special Piedmontese tradition of up to twelve or thirteen tiny first courses, designed to give each diner no more than a mouthful of each different kind of dish. In season try the truffles and/or the mushrooms. Look for seasonal foods, particularly out of Turin, such as game in rich sauces often made from the wines of the region. During the cheese course ask for the restaurant's own version of bross, the fermented cheese cream that various restaurants make in their regional styles.

One of the dishes you should certainly try is a *bagna cauda*, literally a hot bath. It's a hot dip made of a mixture of oil, garlic, anchovies and butter. Sometimes, particularly in the

< 31 >

summer, herbs are added. Autumn and winter time are, without question, an opportunity to enjoy some of the excellent casseroles and stews of Piedmont. The further up towards the Alps you go, the earlier this season really starts, but there are some splendid *brasatos*, the local equivalent of the *stufati* or stews of the rest of Italy, made with whole pieces of meat or game and cooked very slowly and gently until the meat is absolutely falling off the bones but loaded with flavour.

Out of Turin Asti is particularly famous for its food as well as for the fizzy white wine that is named after the town. It is often drunk with pudding courses where its fragrance goes well with the rich pastries and cream based desserts that are so popular. Perhaps the most important advice, when eating out in Piedmont, though, is to go hungry. The quantities seem to be enormous and the number of courses far greater than those you might get in other parts of Italy. There is emerging a new pattern of lighter eating, fuelled particularly by the cosmopolitan nature of much of the social life in Turin itself, and olive oil is creeping in as an alternative to butter as the main cooking ingredient, but indulgence in the good things of life is very much a part of the eating tradition. There are even many shops which specialize in what would be called *traiteur* style service north of the border – shops which supply freshly cooked whole meals to be taken home or occasionally, if you're clever and buy wisely, on a picnic to be eaten as you drive north out of the city up towards the majestic line of mountains that seems to stretch like a curtain across the whole of this dramatic countryside.

Val d'Aosta

< 32 >

AUBERGINE AND COURGETTE FRITTERS

These fritters are extremely simple to make and most delicious on their own or as part of a larger buffet. They are often served in Turin restaurants as part of the *assaggi* or 'tastings' of lots of different delicacies as the *antipasti* course.

Serves 4.

Ingredients

100 g/4 oz tomatoes
2 spring onions, roughly chopped
Pinch each of salt and cayenne pepper
225 g/8 oz each aubergines and courgettes

4 tbsp plain flour
1 tsp garlic salt
½ tsp paprika
6 tbsp olive oil

Method

To make the sauce, place the tomatoes, spring onions, salt and cayenne in a food processor or liquidizer and whizz until blended. You could also finely chop the vegetables by hand and stir in the seasonings, then set aside. Trim the aubergines and courgettes and slice across on the diagonal into 5 mm/¼ in slices. Mix together the flour, garlic salt and paprika in a shallow bowl. Heat the oil in a frying pan on a medium to high heat. Dip the vegetable slices in the flour mixture and fry immediately for 2–3 minutes, turn and fry for another minute. The fritters should be served as quickly as possible. Drain on kitchen paper while you fry the second batch but they should not be kept waiting more than 2–3 minutes after cooking or the crisp coating will suffer. The vegetables should be hot and cooked right through with a crisp shell. Serve at once with the sauce on the side.

BRESAOLA WITH MELON

Bresaola is the air-dried raw beef made high in the Alps near the Swiss border. Rather like Parma ham in texture, it has a salty taste that contrasts wonderfully with the sweetness and juiciness of melon.

Serves 4 as a starter.

< 33 >

Bresaola with melon p. 33

< 34 >

Ingredients

1 medium-sized ripe melon, such as galia or honeydew
1 packet bresaola, about 8 slices
4 tsp fresh lemon juice
4 tsp olive oil
Freshly ground black pepper

Method

Split the melon in half, then cut into quarters and remove the seeds. Peel the hard rind off and cut each quarter into three slices, cutting from the outside to the centre rather like large-scale orange segments. Lay three slices in an attractive pattern on each serving plate, filling in the rest of the plate that is not covered with two slices of the bresaola. Squeeze over a little of the lemon juice. Pour a teaspoon of olive oil in a trail over each plate and grind a little black pepper on top. Chill for up to half an hour before serving.

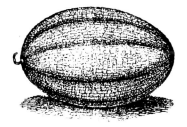

PASTA WITH TRUFFLES

This recipe presumes you have one of the white truffles from Alba. One the size of a large marble will suffice for four people because of the impact of the flavour. If you don't have the truffle, the next best thing is to use a tablespoon of truffle oil in dressing the pasta; add it to the butter in the pan when you melt it.

Ingredients

450 g/1 lb tagliatelle or fettucine egg noodles (*tajarin* in Piedmont)
75 g/3 oz butter   75 g/3 oz parmesan
1 small white truffle (15 g/½ oz)   Black pepper to serve

< 35 >

Method

Put the noodles into a pan of boiling water. If they are soft they will cook in approximately 3 minutes, if dry noodles they will take 3 minutes at the boil followed by 7 minutes standing off the heat with the lid on. In a separate, preferably non-stick, pan melt the butter, add half the parmesan and, if you are using it, the truffle oil. Drain the noodles thoroughly and put them into the pan with the butter and cheese. Turn until thoroughly mixed. If you have a truffle, scrub it thoroughly and grate it finely into the mixture. Turn again, put into a serving bowl and sprinkle the remaining parmesan cheese on top. Serve immediately with plenty of black pepper.

MUSHROOM AND RICOTTA PARCELS

These little pastry parcels look very complicated, but they are actually really easy to make. The pastry I'm using is flaky filo which bakes to a marvellous crisp finish. You can buy it in packets, fresh or frozen. Filo is not traditional but easier to use than the hand-made puff pastry of the region. Ricotta cheese is best in this, or cream cheese as the best alternative.

Serves 4.

Ingredients

225 g/8 oz filo pastry, thawed if frozen
50 g/2 oz butter, melted
2 spring onions, finely chopped
1 tsp each of dried thyme and oregano
1 tbsp chopped fresh parsley
100 g/4 oz ricotta or cream cheese
225 g/8 oz porcini (ceps) or chestnut mushrooms
Salt and freshly ground black pepper
Mixed green salad, to serve

Method

Pre-heat the oven to 350°F/180°C/160°C Fan/Gas Mark 4/bottom of an Aga roasting oven. If the filo pastry comes in oblong sheets, fold them to make squares. If they are

< 36 >

Mushroom & ricotta parcels p. 36

< 37 >

in little squares already, brush one square with melted butter and place another on top so you have double thickness squares. Place the spring onions, the herbs, cheese and seasoning in a bowl and mix well. Take the stalks out of the mushrooms and fill each one with a dessertspoon of cheese mixture. Put a mushroom into the centre of each of the filo pastry squares, brush all round it with melted butter and then pull the corners up and together like a little parcel, twisting the ends together at the top. Arrange on a greased baking tray. Brush all the parcels with a last little bit of melted butter and bake for about 15–20 minutes. Watch them for the last 5 minutes – they are meant to be golden, not burnt! They make a great first course, or, with some other dishes, excellent buffet food.

FONDUTA

This recipe comes from the Alpine region of the Val d'Aosta and it's very similar to the mixture that they eat a little further north in Italian-speaking Switzerland as a fondue. There the trick is to have the thick cheese sauce in a saucepan in the middle of the table and to dip bread and other delicacies into it. In Piedmont, the sauce is likely to be made from fontinà rather than gruyère or emmenthal and to be poured over rice or, in some cases, pasta or polenta rather than have anything dipped into it. It's quite a substantial dish. Serve it in small quantities as a first course or in larger portions as a vegetarian main course.

Ingredients

450 g/1 lb fontina cheese (emmenthal is a good substitute)
4 eggs
300 ml/½ pint of milk
30 g/1 oz butter
Generous teaspoon of cornflour

Method

Cut the cheese into small dice, put in a bowl and cover with the milk. The cheese will absorb a surprising amount of the milk and soften considerably. In a little extra milk slake the cornflour until it's smooth. Add that to the cheese mixture, put it into a non-stick saucepan and heat very gently over a very low heat allowing the cheese to melt.

< 38 >

The cornflour is not traditional but does prevent the mixture curdling. Beat the eggs thoroughly and, off the heat, stir those with the butter into the cheese mixture once it has melted. Stir it all thoroughly to mix but don't let it boil. You can season it with a little white pepper and/or a little truffle oil or even some grated fresh truffles. This amount will deliciously sauce four main course helpings of rice or polenta sliced and grilled, or, although it's not usual, four generous helpings of egg pasta.

BOLLITO MISTO

This dish of mixed boiled meats traditionally has seven ingredients in it, and at that level, unless you happen to have the world's largest cooking pan and a family or appetites to match, is best left to restaurants to prepare. Originally including beef, veal, tongue, chicken, sausages, and quite possibly a calf's foot or pig's trotter, it's a pretty demanding dish to cook. Simplified versions however are extremely popular and indeed it's sometimes simplified so much as to have only one ingredient. The sauces are important. Nowadays they vary considerably, although a green one (see below) is always involved. The Italian community in America often substitute turkey for the veal and I'm going to suggest that as a possible alternative for this simplified home cooked version. Even in this form it's a meal for at least six people with hearty appetites and comes in two courses.

Ingredients

1 boiling fowl (roasting chicken is okay but boiling fowl is better)
1 x 1 kg/2 lb turkey breast joint (or veal shoulder joint)
1.4 kg/3 lb beef brisket in a roll
2 carrots
2 celery stalks
2 medium-sized onions
1 tbsp tomato purée
3 bay leaves
50 g/2 oz celery on the stalk
Sprig of thyme

< 39 >

For the sauce
2 large dill-type pickled cucumbers

1 clove of garlic	1 tbsp capers
1 tin anchovy fillets	50 g/2 oz parsley
2 springs of mint	Juice of 1 lemon
4 tbsp olive oil	1 slice of white bread

Method

In a large pan (a preserving pan is probably the best bet in most households), put 2.4 litres/4 pints of water and the beef and boiling fowl (if you're using a roasting fowl save this until you put in the turkey). The liquid should just cover the meat. Bring it to the boil and skim off any foam or scum that collects on the top. Peel and trim the carrots, trim the celery and cut each stalk in half. Scrub the onions removing any damaged skin but leaving the inner skin on – this will add colour to the broth. Add the vegetables, plus the leaves from the celery and the bay leaf to the dish and simmer gently, covered, for approximately 1½ hours. Add the turkey or veal (and the roasting chicken if that's what you're using) and simmer for another hour until the meats are completely cooked through. Remove the meats from the broth and strain, discarding all the debris. Put the meats back in the strained stock and ladle out enough to make soup as a first course for all the diners. Finely chop the parsley leaves and place a tablespoon in each bowl. Add the rich broth and serve it as a first course. Some people of great appetite add little stuffed pasta hats at this point to the broth. Arrange the meats (you can slice them as you do this) on a large heated platter and serve with boiled potatoes, freshly cooked carrots, some turnips if you like, and the green sauce below. It's also often served with the fruited mustard syrup called Mostada di Cremona which comes from next door Lombardy.

The green sauce
Wash the herbs finely and remove the leaves from the stalks. Put them into a food processor. Cut the gherkins into quarters and add the capers, the peeled and halved clove of garlic, the lemon juice, olive oil, anchovies (with their oil), and the bread, and process until a fairly smooth, coherent mixture is obtained. Some people use mayonnaise instead of the olive oil but it produces too light a flavour for me. Check the balance, it may need a pinch of sugar or a pinch of salt, although the anchovy should have provided quite a lot. If it is too thick add a drop or two of water; if too thin and runny, a little more bread to purée into the mixture.

< 40 >

INVOLTINI

An old-fashioned stuffed beef recipe that's in the tradition of country cooking in the hills around Turin. You may like to flatten the beef slices a little with a mallet or heavy pan to loosen the fibres before rolling them up.

Serves 4–6.

Ingredients

100 g/4 oz fresh white breadcrumbs
1 egg beaten
Large pinch dried thyme and marjoram
50 g/2 oz porcini or ceps mushrooms or shitake
2 spring onions, finely chopped
A little milk (optional)
8 thin slices lean beef (topside is ideal, about postcard size)
2 tbsp butter
1 tsp tomato purée
Salt and freshly ground pepper

Method

Mix the breadcrumbs in a bowl with the egg, herbs and seasoning. Stir in the washed and finely chopped mushrooms and the spring onions. Mix well, adding a little milk if necessary to bind. Place a small spoonful of the mixture at one end of each slice of beef, and roll up. Secure each 'olive' with a wooden cocktail stick, and repeat until you have eight in total. Heat the butter in a large frying pan and quickly fry the beef rolls until just browned all over. Remove from the heat. Add 75 ml/3 fl oz of water and the tomato purée, return to the heat to simmer for 20 minutes until tender. The sauce should be almost dry. Serve hot with sautéd potatoes.

< 41 >

Aubergine & courgette fritters p. 33; involtini p. 41

< 42 >

Hare in sweet & sour sauce p. 44

< 43 >

HARE IN SWEET AND SOUR SAUCE

The ingredients for this may seem outlandish but it's worth remembering that Piedmont is not only famous for its game, but also as the chocolate centre of Italy. The chocolate acts merely as a flavour intensifier on the sauce and you could not identify it if you didn't know what was in there making it so dark and delicious.

Ingredients

1 hare, jointed
1 clove of garlic
2 tbsp red wine vinegar
½ tsp cinnamon
175 g/6 oz each of onions, carrots and celery
4 tbsp olive oil
30 g/1 oz dark bitter chocolate
300 ml/½ pint of beef stock (a cube will do, not Oxo)
50 g/2 oz flour seasoned with ½ tsp ground bay leaf and ½ tsp ground cloves

Method

Mix the flour, cloves and bay leaves together with a little salt, put them into a plastic bag and use to coat the portions of the hare. The legs should be cut into two sections. Heat the olive oil in a oven-going casserole or pan, and fry the hare portions until browned. Peel and chop the onion and carrots finely, chop the celery and the garlic and turn those in the oil with the hare. Turn the heat up to high and pour in the wine vinegar. Allow this to bubble and begin to dislodge the brown crusty bits on the bottom of the pan. Add the beef stock, stir, cover and cook in a low to medium oven, 325°F/160°C/150°C Fan/Gas Mark 3/simmering oven of the Aga, for 1 hour. Remove the pan from the oven. Break up the pieces of the chocolate and stir it into the sauce. If this is reducing too fast, add some more water or beef stock. Add the cinnamon, stirring that into the sauce as well, and turn the hare pieces over. Return to the oven for approximately another half hour. The dark, rich sauce can be puréed and is often served with pasta as a first course, the hare being eaten on its own with sautéd potatoes as a second course, but the pasta and hare go very well together if that's how you prefer to eat them.

< 44 >

EGG AND ALMOND PUDDING

This is known locally as a *tartrà*. They are made in savoury and sweet form and are traditional rustic dishes. This one is comparatively easy to make because the ground almonds act as a binding agent preventing the 'scrambling' of the egg. Traditionally it was often eaten warm, but I find it nicest served in wine glasses as a cream pudding.

Ingredients

600 ml/1 pint of full cream milk (breakfast milk is best)
½ tsp lemon essence (or lemon rind grated with sugar cubes!)
100 g/4 oz caster sugar   4 egg yolks   175 g/6 oz ground almonds

Method

Bring the milk to the boil and add the lemon essence. Beat the eggs and sugar together until they are lemon coloured and fluffy. Stir in the ground almonds and gently pour in the hot, but not boiling, milk, continuing to whisk as you do so. Put back into the saucepan and heat gently until the whole mixture thickens. Try not to boil it, but let it come fairly close to that sort of temperature. Whisk it continuously while you do this. Allow it to cool slightly and pour into wine glasses and chill in the fridge for at least 3 hours before serving. Lemon biscuits go particularly nicely with this.

CHOCOLATE TRUFFLES

This is a home-made version of the hazelnut chocolates that Turin is famous for. They are quite delicious and the hazelnut in the centre is an unexpected and added treat.

Ingredients

225 g/8 oz plain bitter chocolate (high cocoa butter, 70%+ if possible)

30 g/1 oz unsalted butter	**4 tbsp double cream**
The rind of an orange	**2 egg yolks**
1 dozen hazelnut kernels	**2 tbsp cocoa powder**

< 45 >

Method

Put the chocolate, broken up into small pieces, the butter, the double cream and the rind of an orange into a non-stick saucepan and heat very gently until the mixture blends into a smooth consistency. Do not let it boil! Remove it from the heat, add the beaten egg yolks, stir till smooth and pour the mixture into a deep plate. Put it into the fridge until it is set – this should take about 1 hour. Scoop up a dessertspoonful of the mixture, which will now have set but will still be soft and malleable, roll it into a ball, press a hazelnut into the centre of it, and close the chocolate over the outside. Roll each truffle in some of the cocoa powder, place on a piece of greaseproof paper on a plate, and when you have finished all of them (there should be about a dozen), put them back in the fridge to set for at least an hour.

MONTE BIANCO

Why should Italy have a sweet named after a Swiss mountain? For the simple reason that it is an Italian mountain too. Piedmont runs deep into the Alps and claims the south face of Mont Blanc. Then there is the Italians' passion for chestnuts. For chestnut lovers this is perhaps the ultimate dessert. Crafty ones make it, however, with canned chestnut purée to save hours of peeling and sieving.

Serves 4.

Ingredients

175 g/6 oz caster sugar
150 ml/¼ pint of whipping cream
450 g/1 lb unsweetened chestnut purée
100 ml/4 fl oz orange juice
1 tsp vanilla essence

Method

Place the sugar and orange juice in a small pan and heat gently to dissolve the sugar. Remove from the heat. Place the cream in a bowl and whip until thickened but not stiff. Add the vanilla essence to the orange juice mixture and beat in the chestnut purée until smooth. Then with a spoon pile up four 'mountains' on serving bowls. Add a dollop of the cream to make 'snow' on the top of the mountains. Chill for up to 2 hours before serving.

< 46 >

THE VENETO

The north east of Italy, called the Veneto, is one of the most complex regions in this highly complex country. In fact it is three regions rolled together as a result of the extraordinary history of the twentieth century. There is Venice itself, and the Veneto proper which lies between the rivers Po and Tagliamento. In itself it's an amazing and substantial region with, as well as Venice, the great cities of Verona, Vicenza, Treviso and Padua all part of it. Then away to the north, as the Alps climb up towards Austria, there is the Alto Adige or the Trentino, north of the town of Trento. Although definitely a part of Italy now, for three hundred years it was part of Austria and the Austro-Hungarian Empire, and in every way, from language to cooking to traditions, the Tyrolean inheritance is dominant. Away further east, beyond Venice along the Adriatic coast, lies Trieste. Only recently has it and its hinterland, Friuli Venezia Giulia, become a full part of Italy, and its connections to middle Europe and to what used to be Yugoslavia remain very strong. However interesting and significant those two additional parts of the north east of Italy may be, the great city of Venice and its hinterland remain at the heart of the history and traditions both of this part of Italy and of Europe.

Venice has been at the heart of both Mediterranean and European life. Double entry book-keeping was invented there in the twelfth century. Marco Polo left for China from his home in Venice (the front of the house still exists in a tiny square). The murderous first Crusade was launched from Venice by the ancient, blind Doge. Venetian colonies stretched along the north Mediterranean coastline as far as Greece, and the great Venetian galleys traded deep into the Levant for over one thousand years, resisting all conquerors except, briefly, Napoleon. La Seranissima, the great republic of Venice, dominated the Adriatic in every way, and not just in terms of trade. Wealth also brought art. The flowering of the late Renaissance in painting, architecture and sculpture took place in Venice. Venice was also a great home to music, with the early Baroque reaching its apogee under the guidance of the 'red priest' Vivaldi. Its folk arts became legendary, and its carnival, complete with masks and outrageous behaviour, was the early model for the many more tropical versions with which we are more familiar.

Venice was a Republic but that didn't prevent it having a nobility of its own. There was a wonderfully ostentatious lifestyle, caught in many of the paintings of the period. A series of great painters, culminating in Canaletto, documented the extraordinarily complex and highly ritualized

< 47 >

San Marco, Venice

< **48** >

processions and fiestas that the city celebrated on a regular basis. The food too was reputedly as phenomenal and luxurious as the events it was eaten at, but today Venetians believe their cuisine, like that of Florence and Tuscany, is based on simplicity and on the food of the poor. Certainly the dominance of seafood and the necessity to cook as simply as possible has had a strong influence. Local fish and fish products, the spider crab and Baccala Mantacato, which is a salt-cured purée, are great specialities of the region. Monkfish, usually called *rospo*, and scallops are also great favourites, often cooked very simply and sometimes unexpectedly with mint.

Many trading contacts left a legacy of unexpected and exotic combinations of food and flavours. The Po Valley itself however is perhaps most famous in culinary terms for the dominance of polenta, the cornmeal porridge that was wrongly attributed to Turkey when in fact it had come from Mexico in the sixteenth and early seventeenth centuries. After the Second World War polenta fell rather into disrepute as *really* poor people's food, and pasta and rice also grown in the Po Valley became more important. But recently there has been a return to the pleasure of polenta, and it's eaten widely again in the Veneto. Simply cooked, it's mixed with water and salt and boiled until a smooth, golden and very bland substance is obtained. But it's also cooked with milk (occasionally even with wine), with butter, ricotta, and sometimes even sugar and spices. This last reflects an extraordinary Venetian willingness to make in sweet forms what are made as savoury dishes elsewhere. There's a sweet lasagne, a cake made from tagliatelle and sweet rice fritters that are eaten at carnival time mixed with pine nuts, raisins and candied peel. Some meat is eaten, although the Venetians seem to have a preference for offal rather than meat in joints or chops, and their way with liver is famous all over Italy.

There are some other specialities from the inland area. The red chicory or *rosso* comes from there, and in fact there are five different varieties, used in salads, in cooking and as fritters. And it's the town of Treviso that, so recent legend has it, invented Tiramisu, that most popular modern Italian restaurant sweet, literally meaning 'pick me up'. It's made with *mascarpone*, which comes from Lombardy across the Apennines, but the combination of cheese and chocolate, coffee and cake, is typical of the willingness of the people of the Veneto to experiment with ingredients from afar.

< 49 >

Isola di S. Giorgio Maggiore

< 50 >

EATING OUT

The city is dotted with restaurants, cafés and trattoria type inns. There is a simple price rule – the further from St Mark's the cheaper the menu, though the Gritti Palace may be an exception – as expensive as anywhere you can eat. I have always enjoyed the business of wandering in Venice and finding little local places in little squares or courtyards that only the locals visit. The islands of the city, visitable by water bus, offer treats too, especially Murano, Mazzorbo and Burano. There are the sort of eating places where credit cards don't always work, but a smile and enthusiasm does. Look for fish dishes, the light red spider crabs and the various seafood rissottos and shellfish and pasta dishes. There is a very local tradition in some of the wine shops or bars: similar to the Spanish tapas system of snacks to eat with your drink. They start around 11am and run through lunch and open again around 4 in the afternoon.

Further afield above Trento you may find yourself confronting sauerkraut and apfel strudel. Because of the Austrian connection and climate, up in the mountains the food is very much more Germanic while inland it's worth looking for the local specialities. Verona, for example, is famous for its version of potato gnocchi; they even hold a festival for it there at Easter. Treviso specializes in game and Padua is known for its meat in wine sauces. Venetian food doesn't travel that well, the things to eat or drink from, like Murano's famous glass, are much better purchases for the tourist. And so too are the memories, not least one that should be taken home by every visitor, which is a cup of incredibly expensive coffee taken in one of the great cafés that have lined the sides of St Mark's Square since the end of the seventeenth century.

< 51 >

SCAMPI WITH PASTA AND ASPARAGUS

I first had the prototype of this dish in a café overlooking the Mediterranean sea near Trieste. It was marvellous and a must for any scampi and garlic lover. Look for real raw scampi – fresh or frozen – or use tiger prawns as an alternative.

Serves 4 as a starter.

Ingredients

225 g/8 oz rigatoni or any small pasta shapes
75 g/3 oz butter
225 g/8 oz fresh raw scampi or tiger prawns, shelled
100 g/4 oz asparagus tips
2 garlic cloves, crushed
Juice of 1 lemon
Salt and freshly ground black pepper

Method

Cook the pasta in a large pan of boiling salted water for 4 minutes and remove from the heat. Add the asparagus, cover and set aside for 7–10 minutes until the pasta is just *al dente* and the asparagus is just tender. Heat the butter in a heavy-based pan, add the garlic and cook for 10 seconds and then add the scampi. Reduce the heat and cook gently for 2–3 minutes until the scampi are just cooked through and light pink. Drain the pasta and asparagus, add the scampi mixture and lemon juice. Toss to coat and season to taste. Spoon into warmed pasta dishes and serve at once.

ASPARAGUS BASSANO DEL GRAPPA

The asparagus that comes from this wonderfully named town on the edge of the Alps in Veneto is famous for its size and delicacy. It's almost pale white and it's served with a variety of different sauces, most of them based on an egg emulsion of some sort or other. It's often very difficult to find this kind of giant white asparagus, often just tinged with pink in Britain, but buy large, plump asparagus and you will find that the simple mayonnaise that's eaten with them will complement even green versions of the delicious spears.

Serves 4.

< 52 >

Ingredients

675 g/1½ lb large asparagus (approx 4–5 spears each)
2 tbsp white wine vinegar
8 tbsp olive oil (or 4 each of olive and sunflower for a slightly milder flavour)

3 egg yolks
Pinch of salt

Method

Put the asparagus to cook standing up in a pan with the water only just reaching to below the flower heads. Cover and bring to a gentle boil for 15 minutes while you make the mayonnaise. In a food processor or liquidizer, put the egg yolks, the salt, the wine vinegar and a couple of tablespoons of the olive oil. If the asparagus has a slightly bitter flavour you might want to add half a teaspoon of sugar. Put the lid on the machine and process at a high speed for 10–15 seconds. Allow to settle and then process again, pouring the remaining oil in a steady but gentle stream until the mayonnaise thickens. When the asparagus is cooked – test it by putting a sharp knife into the thick part of the base of the stalk – plunge the asparagus into plenty of cold water and allow it to chill down. The intention is not to have it ice cold but to stop it cooking and to cool it to room temperature. Allow it to drain thoroughly in a colander for 4–5 minutes and then place elegantly onto individual plates with the mayonnaise passed to pour over or dip in as individual diners prefer.

GRILLED RADICCIO WITH CHEESE

The bright red and crunchy bitter leaves of red chicory are used in all sorts of ways in the area around their home in the Veneto and there they come in all different shapes and sizes. Here we tend to get the round ones, like miniature cabbages, with quite large white veins. They make, however, delicious bases for a little grilled cheese starter. A variety of cheeses can be used for this but my favourite is fontina, an Italian cheese from the Alps, some of which is made in the Alto Adige, part of the Venetian hinterland. Serve this cooked at the last minute. You can prepare it in advance but it shouldn't go under the grill until everybody is ready to enjoy it.

< 53 >

Grilled radiccio with cheese p. 53

< 54 >

Ingredients

8 generous cup shaped leaves of red radiccio
225 g/8 oz grated fontina cheese (gruyère or emmenthal are alternatives)
1 tbsp grated parmesan
4 tbsp virgin olive oil
Salt and pepper

Method

Place 2 leaves together to form a cup with their stalks pointing in opposite directions. Brush lightly with a little olive oil. Divide the grated fontina into 4 portions and put it into the cups and sprinkle the parmesan on top. Season with salt and generous ground black pepper. Pre-heat the grill, place the radiccio cups, either in heatproof metal dishes or in foil cups which will help them maintain their shape, and grill fairly close to the heat for about 4–5 minutes until the cheese has melted and the leaves are wilted and slightly browned. Remove, pour the remaining oil over the cheese and radiccio and serve immediately. Warn your guests that the filling is extremely hot.

RISOTTO FRUTTI DI MARE

The ingredients for this risotto vary from season to season and fisherman's catch to fisherman's catch. In this country, however, a mixture of squid, prawn and mussels is probably the easiest to achieve. It's absolutely crucial to get risotto rice. This is a medium grain rice sometimes sold as 'arborio', and is the only kind that will absorb the liquid in the right way and form the creamy, smooth texture that Venetians in particular like in their risotto.

Ingredients

900 ml/1½ pints of fish stock (use cubes if you have to)
225 g/8 oz shelled headless tiger prawns or scampi
225 g/8 oz cleaned squid (ask your fishmonger) **450 g/1 lb risotto rice**
1 tbsp white wine vinegar **450 g/1 lb cleaned mussels**
Bunch of spring onions **50 g/2 oz peas (frozen will do)**

< 55 >

Method

Check that the mussels are all closed and unbroken. Put them in a pan with the white wine vinegar and a cup of the stock. Bring to the boil and cover and leave the pan for 3–4 minutes. Discard any mussels that haven't opened, remove the fish from the shells, discarding the shells, and put the resulting liquid back into the stock. Put half of the stock into a large pan and bring it to the boil. Stir in the rice and simmer for about 10 minutes. Add a little more stock and the squid, cut into 1 cm/½ in rings, then after 5 more minutes add the shelled raw prawns and some salt and pepper and stir gently until the fish is cooked and the rice has absorbed all the liquid. You have to judge the risotto for yourself as different rices absorb slightly different amounts of liquid and individual tastes vary. Test a piece of rice – it should be cooked through but still have a little bite at its centre. If it is too dry, add some more liquid, if very runny, either let it cook for a moment or two longer or accept the fact that it's a very Venetian risotto. Finely chop the spring onions and add to the peas (if the peas are fresh they will need to have cooked with the rice from the beginning). Add the mussels, cover and allow to stand, off the heat, for 3 or 4 minutes. Serve in bowls. Normally a spoonful of butter is stirred into each portion and some people like adding grated parmesan cheese, though in Venice it is regarded as strictly out of order.

POLENTA

Polenta is the marvellous maize meal porridge, made in a wide variety of ways, which has finally come back into fashion, not least because it is held to be so healthy. It's only healthy though if it's eaten with other things, as eaten on its own it lacks the vitamins and minerals to keep body and skin healthy. Nowadays it's used in all sorts of ways: as a basis for stews or sliced and grilled. I've even had it cut into chips and dipped in parmesan before being deep fried. It used to be very difficult to make but, as with so many other products, a partly cooked version is available now which needs only about 20–25 minutes cooking rather than the hour or more that it used to. In its homeland polenta comes in fine and coarse, yellow and white, but by and large in Britain it comes in a sort of medium grind and usually yellow. This is ideal for most purposes and the recipe I give here is designed to give you a basic polenta. You can eat it hot with butter and grated parmesan or fontina cheese stirred into it and used rather like mashed potato. Or you can pour it into a dish, about an inch thick, let it cool, slice it, brush it with oil and grill it to accompany roast meats or sausages. You can even try the chips I mentioned above, they were very good though unbelievably calorific.

Serves 4.

< 56 >

Ingredients

350 g/12 oz polenta meal
1½ tsp salt
1.5 litres/2½ pints of water (this quantity is approximate)

Method

Put the water in a large saucepan on a firm base on your stove and bring it to the boil. Add the salt and then put the polenta into a container from which you can pour it easily. Traditionally it was stirred with a paddle-like wooden spoon but a modern whisk is much easier. Pour it in a steady stream into the boiling water, whisking as you go so that lumps don't form. It will very quickly form a thick and quite porridgey dough. It should be possible still to stir it with a whisk, if not, you may need to add a little more water. If it's thin and gruel-like, you may need a little more polenta. Different polentas absorb slightly different amounts of water and only a little testing can tell you. Allow it to cook over a low heat, stirring regularly. I'm afraid this means every couple of minutes making sure that it doesn't burn. Be careful also that it doesn't spit at you and an oven gauntlet while holding the whisk or spoon is a good idea. After about 15–20 minutes (with modern polenta flour) it should start to come away from the sides of the pan and at this point you can pour it into a greased oven tin and slice it and grill or fry it, or if you want to eat it immediately, stir in a generous amount of butter and grated cheese. You may also just stir a little bit into the pan as a whole and then offer more butter and cheese for individual diners to add to their taste. If you have any left over, before it gets cold make sure it gets put into a shape that will allow you to use it grilled or sliced in future as once it's set there's no recovery.

< 57 >

POLENTA WITH LEEK AND SAUSAGE SAUCE

Polenta is eaten widely across North Italy and especially in the Po Valley area where the maize that makes it has been grown for nearly 400 years. It's served in a variety of ways, hot and cold, but one of my favourites is hot with a delicious, rich leek and sausage sauce poured over it, very much as though it were pasta.

Serves 4.

Ingredients

150 g/5 oz fine ground yellow cornmeal or one of the branded polenta mixtures
(this can be 'pre-cooked')
3 tbsp olive oil
450 g/1 lb spicy sausages (I like beef but any good Italian style sausage will do)
400 g/14 oz can chopped tomatoes
450 g/1 lb leeks, cut into 1 cm/½ in slices
1 tbsp tomato purée
1 tsp each oregano, basil and thyme
½ tsp sugar
50 g/2 oz butter
50 g/2 oz freshly grated parmesan

Method

Put 900ml/1.2 litres of salted water on to boil for the polenta. Heat one tablespoon of oil in a large frying pan and gently fry the sausages for 10 minutes until they are browned and firm. Leave to cool a little, then cut into 2.5 cm/1 in pieces. Place the tomatoes and the remaining oil in a separate pan with the leeks and cook gently for 5 minutes. Add the sausage pieces, tomato purée, herbs and sugar. Season generously and simmer for 10–15 minutes. Pour the cornmeal or polenta into the boiling water in one smooth pour, stirring continuously. Continue to stir it over a gentle heat for about 5 minutes for a commercial brand polenta or for about 20 minutes if it is simply cornmeal, stirring every 4 or 5 minutes. Either way, when it's ready it will start to come away from the sides of the pan, then stir in the butter and parmesan. Serve the polenta at once in portions with the leek and sausage sauce spooned on top.

< 58 >

Polenta with leek & sausage sauce p. 58

< **59** >

Coda di rospo p. 61

< **60** >

CODA DI ROSPO

Rospo in Italian means 'toad' and it's because of the extreme ugliness of the head of this fish, which we know as the monkfish, that it got its name. The tail of it, the coda, is however one of the great luxurious fish tastes as it has virtually no bone in it, only a central cartilage, and is as meaty and rich as lobster tail. It's cooked in a variety of ways in Venice but one of the most interesting uses saffron as the main flavouring and mint to add an unusual piquancy. There is a version that's cooked with cream sauce using these two flavours, but I find the mixture slightly unpalatable and therefore suggest the lighter version below, which is closer, I think, to the original than the cream enriched hotel haute cuisine.

Ingredients

1 x 675 g/1½ lb monkfish tail, cleaned and split into 2 halves, cartilage removed
2 tbsp olive oil
150 g/6 oz onion, finely chopped
1 tbsp each of white wine vinegar, raisins and pine nuts
Small packet of saffron powder
Sprig of mint
Salt and pepper

Method

Score the fillets of monkfish crosswise at 2.5 cm/1 in intervals, cutting halfway through the thick end to allow the fish to cook evenly, as it tapers dramatically. Heat the oil in a pan into which both fillets will go and stir in the saffron powder. Turn the fish fillets in the brightly coloured oil, add the onions, cover and allow to cook gently together for about 10 minutes until the fish is just cooked through. Remove to a serving platter. Add the vinegar, raisins and pine nuts to the sauce, season with salt and pepper and bring the sauce to the boil. Pour the sauce carefully over the fish, making sure some of it goes into the deeper cuts. Finely chop the mint and sprinkle over the fish immediately before serving.

< 61 >

CHICKEN COOKED WITH SAGE

The Venetians are very fond of all kinds of poultry and fowl, particular water fowl, and duck, but they're also very good at cooking chicken in very simple ways and when sautéd with sage it makes a very delicious light meal.

Ingredients

1 x 1½ kg/3½–4 lb chicken, cut into 8 serving portions (discarding the central carcass)
Juice of 1 lemon (or 2 tbsp verjuice, white unripe grape juice)
2 tbsp olive oil
2 tbsp flour
50 g/2 oz butter
8–10 fresh sage leaves
Salt and pepper

Method

Dust the chicken pieces with flour and sauté them in half the butter, heated in all the oil, in a sauté pan. Fry them skin side down first for about 8–9 minutes until golden and then turn over. Cook for another 4–5 minutes. Add the lemon juice or the grape juice (verjuice was a very common ingredient all over Europe in the Middle Ages and is still used in parts of the Veneto) and all but 2 of the sage leaves. Cover and allow to cook gently for another 10 minutes. Remove the chicken, discard the cooked sage leaves, season the chicken generously, and put the fresh sage leaves, torn into little pieces, over it. Add the butter to the pan, melt and pour the rest of the juices over. Some people deglaze the pan with a little water or wine to make the juices go further. This goes well with polenta or rice.

< 62 >

FUGAZZA

There's no great tradition of fancy desserts in the Veneto, though there is a species of flat cakes under the generic name of *'fugazza'*. They're cooked at different times of year to celebrate different Saints Days and there is a version left for the Italian equivalent of Mother Christmas, who is supposed to come down the chimney with her bag of presents on Twelfth Night. Like a lot of Italian cakes though they don't seem to travel terribly well but there is a polenta version from Treviso, that Marcella Haazan discovered. It's really a kind of soft biscuit with lots of goodies inside it. This is my version.

Ingredients

100 g/4 oz dried figs, hard stalk removed and cut up into 1 cm/½ in pieces

225 g/8 oz polenta (cornmeal)	**1 tsp salt**
1 tbsp olive oil	**75 g/3 oz caster sugar**
1 tbsp each pine nuts and raisins	**40 g/1½ oz butter**
1 egg	**100 g/4 oz plain flour**
1 tbsp fine white breadcrumbs	**450 ml/¾ pint of water**

Method

Bring the water to the boil in a saucepan with a pinch of salt. Add the cornmeal as though you were making polenta. I stir it with a whisk although wooden spatulas are more traditional. When the cornmeal has turned into a smooth mixture, add the remaining salt and the oil. Let it cook gently until it leaves the side of the pan, about 15–20 minutes. Add the caster sugar, pine nuts, raisins, chopped figs, butter and the egg, beaten in a separate bowl, to the polenta and mix thoroughly. Sieve the flour in and mix until the whole lot is well amalgamated. Butter the sides and bottom of a 22 cm/9 in cake tin, preferably with removable bottom. Scatter in the breadcrumbs and shake round so that they act as a coating. Pour the cake mixture into the tin and smooth down across the top. Bake at 400°F/200°C/180°C Fan/Gas Mark 6/bottom of the Aga roasting oven, with a piece of greaseproof paper over the top for approximately 40–45 minutes. The cake will, surprisingly, rise quite a bit. Remove from the oven and while it is still warm take away the sides of the tin. Turn it upside down on a plate and remove the base as well. Leave it to cool on a wire rack. It's a rich and filling confection and should be served in narrow wedges.

< 63 >

TIRAMISU

Tiramisu has been the fashionable pudding of the early 90s and uses mascarpone cheese, though full fat cream cheese is a good alternative. Despite the north Italian provenance of the essential cheese it's in Treviso that this dish is supposed to have first emerged. This is my own crafty version as there are almost as many tiramisu recipes as there are cooks to make them. It makes a small attempt to control the calories by using some yoghurt.

Serves 4–6.

Ingredients

2 eggs

150 g/5 oz thick Greek yoghurt

½ tsp vanilla essence

10 amaretti biscuits

250 g/9 oz mascarpone cheese

25 g/1 oz caster sugar

1 tbsp instant coffee granules

50 g/2 oz plain chocolate, grated

Method

Separate the eggs and mix the yolks with the mascarpone and yoghurt to a smooth paste in a large bowl. Beat in the sugar and vanilla essence until the mixture is smooth and glossy. Whip the egg whites in a separate bowl until stiffened and fold into the mascarpone mixture. Dissolve the coffee in three tablespoons of boiling water. In a bowl roughly break up the amaretti biscuits. Sprinkle over the coffee and stir until well soaked. Put a layer of biscuits into a large glass serving bowl, spoon over a layer of the mascarpone mixture, put another layer of amaretti on top and finish with a layer of the mascarpone mixture. Sprinkle the grated chocolate on top to cover completely. Chill for at least an hour and up to six. Serve straight from the fridge.

< 64 >

GENOA & LIGURIA

y most vivid memory of Genoa is arriving late one evening, after dark had fallen, and descending what seemed almost like a ring of giant steps down through the city to the port, squeezed into a narrow strip of land next to the sea. In daylight both the city and the surrounding province of Liguria give the same impression, huge terraces dropping down to the deep, clear sea. The area runs from the French border along the coast down to Tuscany, but in shape is really very much like a banana; long and thin and curved, with its own bits of the Alps and Apennines running almost down to the sea edge along most of the coastline. This makes for a very dramatic appearance visually and also, because the inside curve of the banana faces almost due South, a very warm and luxurious climate. Although there isn't much fertile land between the mountains and the sea, and indeed in some places none at all as the cliffs soar high out of the blue and aquamarine water, what there is is very fertile, and the area is famous for its vegetables and fruits.

Genoa's history is very much bound up with the sea. It was one of the two great maritime republics which dominated the Mediterranean; where Venice looked East, Genoa looked South and West. The most famous westward explorer of all time, Christopher Columbus, was a son of Genoa, where his Italian name, Cristobal Coloñ, is celebrated in avenues and statues. Although the city remains Italy's premier port, it's the little villages to the North and South (or rather East and West) along the two halves of the Italian Riviera that attract most attention. The beaches of the area are famous, as are the exquisite little fishing villages like Porto Fino and Alassio. The part of the Riviera that runs up to Ventimiglia, on the French border, is also known as the Riviera of Flowers, as it is a great flower growing centre specializing, amongst other things, in carnations. To the South and West the Riviera di Levante is rockier, though the

beaches, when you come upon them, are equally beautiful. Both rivieras are these days heavily overcrowded in summer by both Italian and Northern European tourists, but still boast a number of small, fine towns which, out of season, carry some of the air of Edwardian grandeur and leisure that they were famous for in their heydays.

Although the coastal restaurants specialize in fish, especially as that is what so many tourists both expect and demand, the traditional cooking of the region centres far more heavily on vegetables. The locals account for this with the fact that after weeks, if not months, at sea, returning sailors wanted the green things of the land rather than the

< 65 >

Liguria

< 66 >

frutti di mare. What is certainly true is that green sauces and vegetables do dominate the traditional local cuisine, and fruit, especially peaches and apricots, are superb and everywhere.

There is not a lot of meat cooking. Some chicken is used, a little veal, often the speciality dish being made from the cheaper, or poor people's cuts, and one or two beef dishes cooked with the famous *funghi porcini* or, as we would know them, wild mushrooms, do exist. But the most famous dish of all in Genovese cooking, and not one to be tried outside the region unless you are either brave or very experienced, is the Capon Magro, literally translated as a thin chicken but in fact containing no meat at all. It is a sort of lenten dish, but rich enough in its own right for all that. There are layers of vegetables, cooked fish with green herbs, nutted cheese sauces all topped with raw shellfish, such as oysters, and cooked slices of lobster.

While there are a number of dishes which hint of the trading nature of the city's past, the food is remarkably free from spices, although the Genovese did trade into the Middle and Far East and, for a while at least, attempted to compete with Venice. Chickpeas are one of the imports that have left a lasting impression. There is a tradition of a kind of giant flat bread, called *farinata*, made of chickpea flour with oil and seasoning. It's still made in some of the old working man's wine bars and cafés near the port. It comes hot and is very filling. So too is the other flat bread for which Genoa is famous, *focaccia*, a wheaten bread now made across much of Italy and flavoured with a variety of toppings, which may be as simple as a sprinkling of coarse salt, or as complex as a pizza. It's really a very close relation of the *pissaliedière* of Nice.

Without question, however, the most dominant culinary theme in Ligurian and Genovese cooking is basil. It's not the only herb for which the Genovese have a passion, but it is the one for which they have the greatest love. It's used in all sorts of ways in the cooking of the region, but central to that cooking, and almost a theme of it, is pesto – the thick green sauce or condiment made from basil, garlic, olive oil and cheese, mixed and pounded with pine nuts. The cheese can be either parmesan or pecorino, the hard and salty sheep's milk cheese that now comes from Sardinia but may well originally have come from Corsica, an island not very far from the Ligurian coast. Pesto appears in everything: stirred into soups, as a dressing for pasta, as a stuffing for the many various pastas and pancakes of which the local people are so fond, and mixed into gravies. The only thing I've not tasted it in, in the region, is in puddings, and that's not least, I suspect, because there aren't many of those. The area is famous for fruits, particularly peaches, apricots and citrus fruits. It's quite hard to find any local recipes for puddings, apart from an extraordinary one for fried custard. This is rather more delicious than it sounds, though it does take some careful handling if you want to make it at home. If you visit the Italian Riviera, do take the time to visit the rather industrial port city of Genoa – rich in atmosphere and with its strong local traditions. A few hours on the waterfront can be pleasant and delicious, as it's there, most of all, you will find the traditional foods of the ancient republic still held in esteem and on plates.

< **67** >

Camogli

< **68** >

EATING OUT

The coastal area around Genoa is perhaps most famed for its dramatic beauty. But it's often inland from the coast you'll need to go if you want to find authentic cooking. As with so many of the beautiful little fishing villages and towns in Italy that have become tourist centres, the cooking in the waterfront cafés, bars and restaurants very much suits the fashionable and particularly the yachting crowd. They expect grilled fish as the centrepiece of their meals when in sight of the briny. It's inland you will find wonderful trays of antipastos, and the famous stuffed vegetables – vegetables of all sorts, peppers, onion, courgettes, courgette flowers, mushrooms – dishes for which the region has a formidable reputation. There too you will find some of the more extraordinary dishes like lettuces stuffed with ricotta and simmered in a soup broth. Home-made pastas can be found here, often made with unusual ingredients, both chestnut and chickpea flour being pressed into use as pasta materials. There will, of course, be fish, but often cooked in unusual ways. Squid with a marvellous potato and tomato sauce, at Easter time a Torta Pasqualina appears filled with cheese, eggs and artichokes and covered in layers and layers of puff pastry. Then perhaps the local way with salt cod, a great maritime standby. It's here too you may well find the famous green minestrone or minestra, always eaten with a spoonful of pesto stirred in. There is also an interesting speciality of the local thin asparagus, wrapped in a delicate pancake and eaten with an unusual, slightly mustard flavoured, hollandaise sauce. There are few culinary delights to take home if you are a tourist. Some of the pecorino cheese for making pesto at home is worth having, and indeed these days, you can buy pesto made locally to take with you as well. It's worth looking out too for the walnut version of pesto (though there are recipes for both later on) and of course these days Britain's supermarkets are well supplied with this especially Genovese speciality.

< 69 >

PESTO

Although it's possible to buy pesto in a number of varieties these days, it's one of those things that's both satisfying and worth making yourself for the flavour. The ingredients take a little gathering but not so much as they used to. There are all kinds of minor variations in how this is made; some people emphasizing more basil, some people using different cheeses, a mixture of pecorino or parmesan, some others adding more or less garlic. Here is a basic simple mixture that you can make quickly in a food processor. Now all the great recipes for pesto tell you to make it by hand in a pestle and mortar. I'm afraid, however, that while I'm sure that this is the correct way, and may add a nuance to the finished dish, the difference between freshly made pesto, even in a food processor and any bought version, is so great I'm willing to bypass the totally handcrafted version myself.

Ingredients

1 big handful basil leaves (an imprecise measure, but a realistic one anyway, they can be big or small leaves but should fill two hands very comfortably, not squeezed tight)

100 g/4 oz parmesan (or pecorino, or half and half)

2 cloves of garlic

Juice of half a lemon or 1 tbsp white wine vinegar

75 g/3 oz pine nuts

150 g/6 oz virgin olive oil

½ tsp salt

Method

Put the basil and the olive oil, the lemon juice or vinegar and the salt in a food processor or liquidizer. Switch on and chop until the basil is fairly finely distributed through the oil. Rough grate the cheese and add that and the pine nuts, and the peeled and roughly chopped cloves of garlic. Blend again until the mixture is fairly smooth but still flecked with green. Taste for balance – it may need a little more salt and a touch more lemon juice and, even though it is slightly sacrilegious, a pinch of sugar. When the mixture is finished it should be bright green. It can be stored in the fridge in sterilized bottles or jars for three or four weeks without serious deterioration, if you pour a little more olive oil on the top to act as a seal.

< 70 >

Pesto p. 70; walnut sauce p. 72

< **71** >

WALNUT SAUCE

This is an alternative to pesto made with similar intent but rather different flavours. The lack of basil is the principle difference, though the sauce is often used in similar ways as a sauce for pasta, particularly stuffed pasta like ravioli, and sometimes on fish. There are recipes for making a basil sauce with walnuts instead of pine nuts too. So you can experiment quite legitimately.

Ingredients

1 slice of white Italian style bread, cut 2.5 cm/1 in thick
225 g/8 oz walnut pieces (shelled)
1 clove of garlic
100 g/4 oz parmesan
150 ml/6 fl oz olive oil
Salt and pepper
150 ml/¼ pint milk or water

Method

Take the crust off the bread and reduce it to breadcrumbs in a food processor. Add enough milk or water to soak it completely (milk makes for a softer tasting sauce). Add the walnuts and the peeled and roughly chopped garlic and the olive oil and process thoroughly. Season with salt and pepper and stir in the parmesan. This will keep in the fridge in a sealed sterilized jar for up to two weeks.

TOMATO SALAD WITH PESTO DRESSING

This salad is dressed with a version of pesto sauce, a speciality of that bit of the Mediterranean that runs round from Nice in France and down to Genoa in Italy. It's made with slight variations along the coast. All versions however share a particular affinity with tomatoes, as does the basic herb basil, itself.

Serves 4 as a starter.

< 72 >

Tomato salad with pesto dressing p. 72

< 73 >

Ingredients

450 g/1 lb tomatoes, large or small, but ripe!

25 g/1 oz fresh basil plus extra to garnish

40 g/1½ oz freshly grated parmesan or pecorino

Salt and freshly ground black pepper

Crusty bread, to serve

50 g/2 oz pine nuts

120ml/4 fl oz olive oil

1 garlic clove, chopped

2 tbsp white wine vinegar

Method

Slice the tomatoes, if large, into 5 mm/¼ in thick slices and lay them in an attractive pattern in a shallow china dish. If using cherry tomatoes, halve these and place in the same sort of container. Place the pine nuts in a small frying pan and dry-fry for 3–4 minutes, stirring occasionally until golden. Leave to cool a little, then place them in a food processor or liquidizer with the basil, oil, garlic, parmesan, vinegar and seasoning and process until a smooth green purée. Drizzle the pesto dressing over the tomatoes and leave to marinate for at least half an hour – up to 2 or 3 hours in the fridge is fine. Garnish with a few reserved basil leaves.

STUFFED MUSHROOMS

This method of stuffing mushrooms can be extended to other vegetables too, like large hollowed out onions or courgettes, big enough to be turned into canoes. In Liguria you often get a range of three or four different stuffed vegetables as an antipasto. Very rarely do they have meat in them, but the stuffing can include a variety of other ingredients, including ricotta, and, when it's not mushrooms being stuffed, mushrooms themselves.

Ingredients

4 large open field type mushrooms 7.5 cm/3 in plus across

50 g/2 oz grated parmesan or pecorino cheese

1 tbsp finely chopped parsley

½ tsp salt with a clove of garlic crushed into it

50 g/2 oz breadcrumbs

1 ripe tomato

1 egg

4 tbsp olive oil

1 tsp pesto

< 74 >

Method

Take the stalks out of the mushrooms. Put them and the mushroom caps into a colander and pour over a kettle of boiling water. Chop the stalks roughly and add to the garlic and salt, the breadcrumbs, half the cheese, the olive oil and parsley and pesto. Chop the tomato finely and add that and mix together with the egg. Use to fill the mushroom caps. Sprinkle over the remaining olive oil and cheese and place on an oiled baking dish, into which they just fit. Bake in a medium oven, 375°F/190°C/170°C Fan/Gas Mark 5/bottom of the roasting oven of the Aga, for approximately 20 minutes, until the mushrooms are cooked but not too wilted. Serve hot or cold. A little extra parsley over the top always looks good.

SPINACH WITH PINE NUTS AND RAISINS

A simple way to cook spinach, with an interesting sweet and sour tang with the crunchiness of the pine nuts suggesting a geneaology from the eastern Mediterranean.

Ingredients

675 g/1½ lb fresh spinach
1 tbsp olive oil
2 tbsp raisins

25 g/1 oz butter
50 g/2 oz pine nuts
½ tsp ground nutmeg

1 lemon, quartered

Method

In a large pan bring plenty of salted water to the boil. Plunge in the spinach, bring the water back to the boil and cook for about 2 minutes. It should still be bright green, but thoroughly soft. Drain well in a colander and make one or two cuts across the leaves with a knife to help all the surplus water run out. Heat the butter gently in a pan and turn the spinach in the butter. In a separate pan, place the oil and the pine nuts and cook gently until the nuts are golden in colour. Be careful not to let them burn or cook too long. Allow them to cool slightly. Mix the raisins and nutmeg into the spinach and turn it into a warmed oval or round gratin dish. Sprinkle the pine nuts on top and serve with lemon quarters to squeeze over each serving.

< 75 >

Focaccia p. 77

< 76 >

FOCACCIA

Focaccia is related to pizza in that it is a flat bread with tasty toppings, baked, if possible, in a brick oven, but there the resemblance ends. It's meant to be eaten as bread rather than as a dish in its own right, and although it may have flavourings and be used as a snack with a glass of wine, it's the dough itself that's central to the activity rather than being there simply to carry all kinds of other goodies on top of it. It's flavoured with coarse sea salt right the way through to finely grated cheese with black olives. My own favourite adds some sun-dried tomatoes and a fine sprinkling of rosemary to the coarse sea salt . You need strong bread flour for this easy-to-make bread.

Ingredients

450 g/1 lb strong bread flour
225 g/8 oz warm water (approx)
15 g/½ oz fresh yeast (or ½ packet dried yeast)
50 g/2 oz sun dried tomatoes in oil

Pinch of sugar
3 tbsp olive oil
1 tsp coarse sea salt
1 tsp rosemary sprigs

Method

If using fresh yeast mix it with the sugar and a tablespoon or two of the warm water taken from the measured quantity and allow it to froth up in a little basin for about 5–10 minutes. If using dried yeast, mix it in with the flour. Then mix the flour, (the fresh yeast if you are using it) and the water together with the olive oil and knead until the dough has a springy consistency. By hand this should take 2–3 minutes, in a food processor about 45 seconds. Roll the dough into a ball, add a little more olive oil on the surface to stop it sticking, put it in a basin, cover with a tea towel and leave in a warm, draught-free place for about half an hour to an hour until it has roughly doubled in size. Knock it back with your hand and knead for another 35 seconds to a minute. Spread out into a large, flat, thin rectangle – you can do this with a rolling pin but I find hands are just as easy – on to a lightly oiled baking sheet. Press all over the surface of the bread with your fingertips to make little dents. Sprinkle the coarse salt and the rosemary over the top, finely chop the sun-dried tomatoes and sprinkle them, finishing by tipping their oil over the bread as well. Leave to prove for another 30 minutes. It should rise up to be about a maximum of 1 cm/½ in thick. Bake in a hot oven, 400°F/200°C/190°C Fan/Gas Mark 6–7/top of the Aga roasting oven, for about 15–20 minutes until it's golden brown. Don't let it cook too much – it's too thin to be allowed to go crisp. Serve it hot from the oven if you can.

< 77 >

LAMB WITH ROCKET

Rocket, or aruglia, is a green vegetable halfway between spinach and watercress in flavour. It used to be eaten a lot in Britain in past centuries but, until recently, it went out of favour. It is one of the distinctive vegetables eaten with lamb and sometimes with chicken in Liguria. This is a very simple but very robust way of dealing with both the lamb and the rocket which is available these days in most supermarkets and greengrocers. I had it served in my favourite Ligurian restaurant with mashed potatoes made with olive oil rather than butter. I don't know if that is a traditional dish of the region, but it certainly went well with my lamb.

Ingredients

8 thick cut lamb chops (butterfly if possible)
2 cloves of garlic
2 tbsp olive oil
225 g/8 oz rocket leaves
Juice of half a lemon
Salt and pepper

Method

Peel and crush the garlic with the blade of a knife or a garlic press. Mix it with half the oil and rub it over the lamb chops. Leave for at least half an hour, up to 12 hours is fine. Heat a grill very hot (line the pan with foil for easy cleaning and reflective heat) and grill the chops for 6–8 minutes a side, depending on whether you like your lamb pink or cooked through. Brush them with the garlic oil marinade when you turn them. Meanwhile in a small frying pan heat the remaining oil and stir-fry the rocket leaves, which you should have washed and not dried too thoroughly. If they are very large, cut them in half. Fry them quickly while the lamb is grilling, stirring almost continuously until they have wilted but not in any way browned. Remove from the heat, squeeze over the lemon juice and season generously. Serve a portion of the quite pungent rocket with the lamb chops and either the mashed potatoes as mentioned above, or any other suitable starch to your taste. A good grinding of black pepper over both the chops and the rocket leaves is traditional.

< 78 >

RICE AND SPINACH TART

This is an unusual way of using both rice and spinach, making it into a kind of savoury cake without any pastry around it. It's very simple but does need the arborio or risotto rice that is used in most North Italian recipes. There are versions of this made with a mixture of herbs: mint, basil, oregano and parsley all chopped up together, but I prefer the simplicity of the spinach one. It can be eaten cold and is quite favoured by families from the south of the region as picnic food.

Ingredients

675 g/1½ lb fresh spinach, free of coarse stalks
1 large onion
225 g/8 oz arborio rice
3 eggs
150 g/6 oz parmesan
50 g/2 oz butter
½ tsp ground nutmeg and black pepper
½ tsp salt

Method

Wash the spinach thoroughly and cook it in a little boiling, salted water until it softens. Place it in a colander to drain and chop at it with the back of a knife or a wooden spatula until as much of the liquid as possible is out. Squeeze till quite dry. In the same pan, with a little extra water, boil the rice for about 10 minutes until it's just done, with a bit of bite at the centre. Drain it and mix with the spinach. Peel and very finely chop the onion and sauté gently in the butter until it's transparent. Mix that, the parmesan finely grated, the eggs, the pepper, salt and nutmeg together with the rice and spinach. Butter a 20 cm/8 in cake tin (preferably one with a removable bottom) and press the rice and spinach mixture into it, smoothing down the top. Bake at 400°F/200°C/190°C Fan/Gas Mark 6/middle of the roasting oven of the Aga, for about 30 minutes until the top is golden. Remove carefully (it breaks quite easily) from the tin and serve immediately hot with a tomato sauce, or cold as picnic finger food.

< 79 >

POLLO ALLA CAMPAGNA

This dish has parallels all over northern Italy and as its name indicates is a particularly rustic dish in a cuisine of rustic dishes. The sweet fennel sausages which are used for this are virtually unobtainable in Britain. I find the coarse cut 'butchers' style beef sausages recently relaunched here make an excellent substitute. This is a filling one-dish meal.

Serves 4–6.

Ingredients

225 g/8 oz coarse cut 'butchers' beef sausages (or Italian sweet fennel sausages)
1 whole chicken, cut into 8 pieces (or 8 portions)
225 g/8 oz onion, chopped
450 g/1 lb ripe or canned plum tomatoes, chopped
2 tbsp olive oil
2 garlic cloves, crushed
1 bulb fennel
225 g/8 oz mixed mushrooms, such as ceps, chestnut and shitake
Crusty bread, to serve

Method

Heat the oil in a large pan and fry the chicken pieces over a high heat until browned all over. Reduce the heat and add the onion and garlic and mix until they are well coated in the oil. Cut the sausages into 2.5 cm/1 in lengths and add them to the pan with the tomatoes. Season to taste and simmer for 25 minutes. Meanwhile, cut the fennel into 1 cm/½ in cubes, reserving the feathery green fronds. Then add the fennel and mushrooms to the pan and simmer for another 10 minutes. Season generously and ladle into wide rimmed serving bowls and sprinkle over the reserved fronds. You could eat this with pasta or potatoes but I prefer crusty bread to mop up all the wonderful juices.

< 80 >

Pollo alla campagna p. 80

< 81 >

ORANGES IN CARAMEL

All over the world Italian restaurants' sweet trolleys carry a few classic dishes and among them is a bowl of golden oranges in a deep golden sauce. No one is certain where the dish actually began, but Liguria is a favourite with its contacts with Spain, North Africa and the Eastern Mediterranean. Only eat it with cream if you must. It's better without!

Serves 4.

Ingredients

4 large oranges   50 g/2 oz caster sugar   450 ml/¾ pint water

Method

Carefully peel two of the oranges removing as little of the pith as possible, then cut into matchsticks. Place in a pan with 300 ml/½ pint of water and bring to the boil. Then drain, discarding the water. Melt the sugar with one tablespoon of water in a small heavy-based pan. Simmer gently until the mixture is pale gold and smells like toffee. Remove from the heat and add the remaining 150 ml/¼ pint of water stirring continuously until the caramel is completely dissolved. Stir in the blanched peel. Peel the remaining two oranges and cut each into six slices. Arrange in an attractive pattern on a shallow serving dish and pour over the caramel sauce. Chill for at least an hour before serving.

< 82 >

LATTE DOLCE FRITO

This extremely unusual dish is a great speciality of the coast, though no-one seems to be able to tell me why. There are, as always with these things, a number of versions, but this one seems to have the safety of an adequacy of cornflour blended into the custard to make sure it doesn't collapse too readily when it's been fried. Traditionally, these little rissoles are deep fried but I think they work better, and are more controllable if you shallow fry them in about 1 cm/½ in of vegetable oil. Again, tradition has olive oil but I find that too strong a taste with these sweet fritters.

Ingredients

450 ml/¾ pint of milk
100 g/4 oz caster sugar
6 egg yolks
5 tbsp cornflour
Grated rind of 1 lemon
1 tsp vanilla essence
1 of the egg whites
2 slices white bread reduced to breadcrumbs

Method

Whisk the egg yolks with the sugar and the cornflour. Bring the milk to the boil with the vanilla essence in it. Then, when off the boil, add, stirring and whisking all the time, to the egg yolk and the sugar mixture. Add the lemon rind and cook this mixture very gently in a double boiler or in a basin over hot water for about 20 minutes. The cornflour should stop the mixture separating, but, whatever you do, do not let it boil vigorously. Once it's thick, and it should be very thick, pour it into an oiled, shallow, rectangular tin that, if possible, you have lined with non-stick silicone paper. The custard should be about 2.5 cm/1 in in depth. Leave it to set overnight, preferably out of the fridge. Tip the custard out onto a clean chopping board and cut into 2.5 cm/1 in slices. Whisk the egg white until it's frothy. Dip each slice carefully in the egg white and roll in the breadcrumbs. Fry in oil, 2–3 minutes a side if shallow frying, about 3–4 minutes if deep frying. The outside should be crisp and golden and the inside still soft and creamy. Traditionally they are dusted with icing sugar before serving.

< 83 >

The 1997 Ferrari rally pictured in Radicofani

< 84 >

EMILIA-ROMAGNA

Emilia-Romagna is one of the double-barrelled Italian provinces. Although it's now regarded as a unified area it really is two quite separate regions. Emilia, running from the Apennines to the Adriatic, is the southern flood plain of the Po Valley, flat, rich and agricultural, studded with famous ancient towns like Bologna, Modena, Parma and Ferrara. The Romagna on the other hand is in the foothills and the high mountains of the Appennine chain, a hard country more like the Marches to the south of it than the northern part of its own province.

This double-barrelled province enjoys substantial prosperity (Ferraris are built at Modena) and in addition the agricultural wealth of the region, particularly of Emilia, is enormous and celebrated in its extraordinary rich cuisine. It has long been regarded as the gastronomic centre of Italy, particularly the towns of Bologna and Parma. Salami-type sausages even have the generic name of Bologna taken from that town, and Parma is famous both for its lightly salted pink ham, which has become a universal product around the world and its possibly even more famous cheese – parmesan. Both these products are made under strict supervision and licensing, and may only come from certain breeds of animal raised in certain areas and processed in certain ways. The whole area is famous for its salamis and sausages, and almost every other part of the pig is turned into some kind of preserved meat or mortadella. The banks of the Po also produce enormous amounts of soft European-style wheat, not really suitable for the hard dry pastas but perfect for the egg-based pastas made in the area. These are very rich, sometimes so rich that virtually nothing except a little butter and cheese is used to dress them. Dry pasta is virtually unknown here except in some of the poorer student areas. Bologna is the oldest continuous university in Europe having existed since the twelfth century, and even now is crowded with tens of thousands of students whose eating houses bring a touch of restraint and reality to the lush cooking of the region.

The egg pasta is often hand-made and is in many ways a quite recent invention. They also stuff the egg pasta with the most amazing range of fillings and make it into fanciful shapes. Fillings can range from the very simple, a little spinach and cheese, through to complicated meat pastes cooked for hours. Essential to the cooking is the ragù or meat sauce, of which our Bolognese sauce is merely a pale echo. Made in a variety of ways, it usually includes milk or cream as well as the minced meat.

Fish is little eaten inland; on the coast it is caught and eaten

< 85 >

in the many traditional ways of the Italian fisherman. In the cities however meat is king, particularly in the town of Parma where, apart from the hams, the rest of the pig is put to all kinds of uses. It's one of the few places in Italy where fresh pork is eaten as a regular dish. Beef is also popular, using spices as much as herbs to augment the very slow and gentle cooking. Game is eaten, both casseroled and roasted, and the grain-fed chickens are famous throughout Italy. Vegetables on their own play a lesser part here than they do in other parts of the country, usually being cooked with the addition of the ever-present parmesan cheese. In the region this is much more varied in its forms than it is outside, there being young, medium and aged cheeses (the latter being at least three years old) and the younger ones are frequently eaten as cheese in their own right rather than being used for cooking.

Apart from Bologna and Parma, the other cities have some of their own specialities, particularly Modena with its balsamic vinegar. This extraordinary substance, at its peak dark and almost liquorice black, is a recent revival of an ancient technique that was almost lost. The vinegar is made on the 'Solera Method', very like sherry, where a certain quantity of vinegar is drawn off from each barrel and moved into an older one, so that the most ancient barrel never empties but has a chance to add the maturity of its flavours to younger vinegars. Some vinegars are aged as much as eighty years by this method, though they are extremely difficult to come by and mortifyingly expensive when you do. Good ten or twelve year old Balsamico di Modena though is absolutely worth having, and is used as a flavouring as much as a substance in its own right. A couple of drops can transform a salad dressing, a tablespoon can spike a stew, and it's even used in sweet dishes, particularly on fruit like strawberries where its sweet and sour piquancy seems to bring out the flavour rather than drown it.

Further south, in the Romagna, food tends to be simple, particularly as you move up into the mountains. Here the pasta lacks eggs and the cooking lacks the richness and the lavishness of the cities of the plain. Perhaps the most overwhelming style of their cooking is the grill, a habit they share with the Marches people to their south. They grill almost everything: poultry, fish, meat and game, and make a speciality out of *castrato*, mutton from gelded sheep which have very tender and substantial joints. Like other mountain people in the area, they also make a speciality of some of the products that used to be the food of the poor: chestnuts made into cakes and fritters, and fish soups made from the boniest fish in the catch. In many ways the cooking echoes modern styles in that it's 'healthier', being lower in fat and calories than the cooking of Emilia. Bologna, because of the richness of the food there, proudly maintains the title of La Grassa, or 'the fat one', not least due to its famous outdoor eating festivals.

These festivals tend to run through the summer in both the centre and the suburbs of the city, and, if you're in Bologna or its environs at the time, are absolutely not to be missed. It is a chance to taste the greatest cooking in Italy on its home ground.

< 86 >

Bologna

< 87 >

EATING OUT

If you're planning an excursion to a restaurant in the Bolognese, wear loose clothing and leave your calorie counter behind. The richness of the food and the number of the courses is likely to astonish you, unless you go for one of the quite intentional 'light' menus which are becoming much more prevalent these days. Otherwise you're likely to get the full six course meal of the region: a plate of the salted or cooked meats and hams is followed by soup, almost certainly containing some of the extraordinary and intricate stuffed little pastas. Then a dish of the pasta itself, almost certainly rich with eggs, and either served with one of the cream loaded ragù meat sauces or a mixture of butter, cheese and cream. Depending on the season the next course will be either roasted or stewed meat, beef probably in Bologna, pork in Parma, game in Ferrara and chicken almost anywhere. They'll be cooked according to the region too, with the use of eastern spices like cloves or cinnamon in the Bolognese and the famous aged vinegar used as a basis in Modena and its surrounding countryside. Cheese follows, including almost certainly parmesan or one of its winter variants (the real stuff is only made in the summer); then either fruit or a range of pastries, particularly in and around Parma. Particularly popular in most of the restaurant menus are cream puddings, a unique taste in Italy, known often as *Bavarois* or Bavarian creams, with quite fancy ingredients or sometimes very simple ones known as *panna cotta* or cooked cream – simple custards often flavoured with little more than vanilla. I find that an indulgence in all six courses is usually more than the human frame can stand, but it's worth mentioning that there are also seasonal specialities, particularly tomatoes which are wonderful grown in this area. As for mushrooms, they have some unique ones that look like eggs with bright orangey centres, and their own regional versions of some of the great national specialities like Bollito Misto and Fritto Misto. Here, as in so much, the mix tends to be much richer than in other parts of Italy, with mixtures of meat and cheese and truffles bound together in bechamel sauces cut into lozenges or balls, and mini skewers threaded with delicacies like coxcomb before being egged, breadcrumbed and deep fried.

It is possible to eat more economically and more moderately however, particularly in the cities where there is a student population. Here is lighter fare, often derived from the south and cooked by immigrants from other provinces who moved north to take the benefit of the economic prosperity of the area. Here too you will find regional foods as well as slightly simplified forms of the local cuisine. In Ferrara you'll find some traditional cooking from the Jewish style, with goose and goose fat replacing pork and pork fat in a whole range of dishes. There's even a goose ham, Prosciutto d'Oca, and lots of luscious rich and often deep fried snacks, both savoury and sweet.

In a region where cheese and salamis and salted meats are so plentiful, picnics are an obvious pleasure. Fruit is plentiful and very varied, with parmesan cheese to eat in chunks and excellent local bread. Simple eating out can be one of the great culinary pleasures of a region more famed for its sumptuous fare and grand restaurants.

< 88 >

PENNE COL SUGO

This dish is normally made with a spinach flavoured noodle, hollow in the middle and very difficult to find outside Emilia. Penne, the quill-shaped pasta, make an ideal substitute. The sauce is one of the many variants using meat and milk, of which the area is so fond.

Ingredients

1 tbsp olive oil

225 g/8 oz minced veal or chicken

150 ml/¼ pint of milk

½ tsp salt

50 g/2 oz butter

450 g/1 lb penne

100 g/4 oz each onion, carrot and celery

½ tin of Italian plum tomatoes

½ tsp freshly ground nutmeg

100 g/4 oz grated parmesan

Method

Peel, wash and chop the vegetables. Turn them in the oil and add the minced meat. Cook over a moderate heat for about 8 minutes until the vegetables are translucent and the meat is lightly browned. Add the milk, stir it together and leave to simmer over a very low heat for 10 minutes. Add the tomatoes, the salt and spices and simmer, covered, for 40 minutes. If the sauce starts to dry out, add a little water. Cook the pasta in boiling salted water for 3 minutes, allow to stand off the heat covered for another 7–8 minutes. Drain thoroughly and stir in the butter. When that's melted from the heat of the pasta, add the meat sauce, stir thoroughly and serve with plenty of black pepper and the parmesan cheese.

HOME-MADE PASTA

I'm not a great one for home-made pasta, particularly not any that can be reasonably bought, but the simple fact is that fresh egg pasta made with the volume of eggs to flour that is used in the Emilia-Romagna area simply doesn't exist commercially. Suffice it to say that this recipe is comparatively modest, using a pound of flour to 4 eggs. There is a recipe I know of which requires 20 egg yolks to each kilo of flour. This, however, is a revelation in itself and can be eaten with the very simple cream and cheese butter sauce that follows, to get the authentic

< 89 >

Pasta making p. 89

< 90 >

taste of Emilia. Traditionally this pasta is made by hand on a marble slab, I find that a food processor, or perhaps even better, a food mixer, is much the best technique. A pasta machine is fine if you've got one but you can roll it out by hand with a rolling pin and dry it, as my Italian neighbour used to, on tea towels laid over the backs of kitchen chairs.

Ingredients

450 g/1 lb white flour, preferably unbleached but not bread flour
½ tsp salt   **4 eggs**

Method

Sift the flour to remove any lumps, add the salt and place in the bowl of a food processor or kitchen mixer. Switch the machine to 'on' and add the eggs, one at a time, blending at a slow speed. As the eggs go in so the dough will become coherent and cling together. Knead, still at a moderate speed, for 1½–2 minutes (by hand it's 10–15 minutes). If it's too sticky add a little more flour, if it's too dry to cling together, add a little water, by which I mean a teaspoon at a time. Grease it lightly with olive oil and allow it to rest in the fridge or a cool place for about half an hour. On a floured board, using an ordinary rolling pin, roll the dough out until it's 3 mm/⅛ in thick. The shape or regularity of the edges doesn't matter. Allow it to dry on a tea towel for about half an hour, roll each sheet up loosely and cut across into 5 mm/¼ inch ribbons. You now have egg tagliatelle. If you substitute about 100 g/4 oz of cooked, drained and puréed spinach for one of the eggs, you will have spinach tagliatelle. Once the pasta has had a chance to dry a little more, it will cook in boiling salted water in about 2–3 minutes.

To serve:
750 g/3 oz unsalted butter   **225 ml/8 fl oz double cream**
100 g/4 oz parmesan cheese

Drain the cooked tagliatelle and add the butter, stirring it to allow it to melt. Heat the cream in a small saucepan and add half the cheese. Just before it boils, take it off the heat and stir into the pasta. Serve with the rest of the cheese sprinkled on top. Black pepper and a little salt depending on how salty the parmesan is complete the dish. Don't be tempted to add anything else.

< 91 >

RICOTTA AND FENNEL GRATIN

This is a pretty and unusual vegetarian dish and one of the ingredients is also the container for the food. If you can't find ricotta, buy cottage cheese and beat until it's smooth. Sometimes the gratin is made in Modena with the fennel sliced and layered with the ricotta mixture.

Serves 4 as a starter.

Ingredients

2 large fennel bulbs

1 bunch spring onions, chopped

225 g/8 oz ricotta or cottage cheese

1 tbsp olive oil plus extra for greasing

50 g/2 oz pine nuts

1 tbsp chopped fresh basil

Salt and freshly ground black pepper

Method

Preheat the oven to 350°F/180°C/160°C Fan/Gas Mark 4/bottom of an Aga roasting oven. Cut the base off the fennel bulbs and pull the stalks away gently. You should wind up with four large spoon-shaped stalks and a central section of the bulb from each piece of fennel, then chop the remaining centres. Heat the oil in a frying pan and sauté the chopped fennel with the spring onions until softened. Add the pine nuts and cook for another minute to a minute and a half stirring until the pine nuts are pale golden. Leave to cool slightly. Put the ricotta or cottage cheese into a bowl and stir in the fennel and pine nut mixture. Add the basil and season generously. Place the fennel 'spoons' on a lightly oiled baking sheet and spoon the cheese mixture into the centre of the 'spoons', distributing it evenly. Bake for 25–30 minutes until the fennel spoons are softened but not disintegrated and the cheese centre is lightly browned. You can serve these hot from the oven or cold with a little oil and lemon sprinkled over.

< 92 >

Ricotta & fennel gratin p. 92

< **93** >

BOLOGNESE SAUCE

Here are two different versions of the ragù bolognese. Both are quite authentic, indeed the second, less usual, one comes from a Bolognese acquaintance whose party piece it is. Both can be served with tagliatelle or any other long, and preferably, egg pasta. They are also quite okay with spaghetti.

RAGÙ BOLOGNESE I

This is a proper ragù, the original of our 'spag bol' sauce. Use a teaspoon of each of the herbs if you are using fresh. Serve with tagliatelle or use it in a lasagne (see below). Despite claims that it is never eaten with spaghetti, in the hundreds of student cafés in Bologna, and in neighbouring towns, the cheaper option of spaghetti with the sauce is often found.

Serves 4.

Ingredients

100 g/4 oz chicken livers, thawed if frozen and chopped

2 tbsp olive oil	450 g/1 lb minced beef
1 large onion, finely chopped	1 garlic clove, finely chopped
1 carrot, grated	400 g/14 oz can Italian chopped tomatoes
1 tbsp tomato purée	½ tsp each freeze-dried oregano, thyme and basil
2–3 tbsp double cream	Salt and freshly ground black pepper

Method

Heat the oil and fry the beef until lightly browned. Add the onion, garlic and carrot and continue to fry for 3–4 minutes. Add the tomatoes and tomato purée, season generously and simmer for a further 15–20 minutes with the saucepan partly covered. Add the chicken livers and herbs, plus a little water. Cook for a further 15–20 minutes until the sauce is well blended. Add two to three tablespoons of thick cream before serving the sauce with pasta and parmesan.

< 94 >

RAGÙ BOLOGNESE II

This recipe is decidedly unusual in that the beef is simmered in milk for hours, however it is 'authentic', having come from a Bolognese woman taught it by her mother! It makes a gentler, almost sweet, rich sauce.

Ingredients

450 g/1 lb lean minced beef
1 stick celery, finely chopped
½ tsp dried thyme
1 bay leaf
1½ tsp salt
1 tsp dried oregano

225 g/8 oz onion, finely chopped
1 medium carrot, peeled and finely chopped
1 clove garlic, peeled and left whole
1 tbsp sun dried tomato paste or tomato purée
1.2 litres/2 pints semi-skimmed milk
2 cloves garlic, peeled and chopped

1.4 litres/48 fl oz (2 large bottles) chopped tomatoes or passatta
Freshly ground black pepper

Method

Put the mince, onion, celery, carrot, chopped and whole garlic, bay leaf and tomato purée into a heavy-bottomed large saucepan. Pour over the milk and stir to break up the meat. Cook over a gentle heat, stirring occasionally until the milk has evaporated and the meat almost 'fries' again. This is a slow process taking up to 2 hours depending on the heat under the pan. The meat will become very soft from such slow cooking and the finished sauce more delicious. Once the milk has evaporated remove the bay leaf and whole clove of garlic. Add the salt, herbs and tomatoes, and season with pepper. Stir well and cook over a low heat for a further 50 minutes to 1 hour, stirring occasionally until you have a rich bolognese. Bolognese sauce is best mixed into pasta rather than spooned on top and served with freshly grated parmesan cheese.

< 95 >

LASAGNE VERDE

You can make this famous dish using one of the ragùs detailed above. Here though is a lighter version of the dish with chicken livers instead of beef. If you want a vegetarian version, you can leave out the chicken liver, in which case add the same amount of Florentine-style fennel cut into 1 cm/½ in thick slices and cooked in the same way. This dish has three simple stages to it to build up a delicious layered confection. The soaking of the pasta sheets removes the need to boil them.

Serves 4–6.

Ingredients

350 g/12 oz chicken livers, thawed if frozen
3 tbsp crème fraîche or double cream
200 g/7 oz chopped tomatoes
Salt and freshly ground black pepper
40 g/1½ oz freshly grated parmesan

1 onion, finely chopped
100 g/4 oz mushrooms, sliced
40 g/1½ oz plain flour
75 g/3 oz butter
450 ml/¾ pint of milk

225 g/8 oz lasagne verde, soaked in warm water for 5 minutes
175 g/6 oz frozen spinach, defrosted and squeezed dry

Method

Preheat the oven to 350°F/180°C/160°C Fan/Gas Mark 4/bottom of an Aga roasting oven. Heat half the butter in a frying pan and add the chicken livers, onion and fry until the onion has softened. Add the mushrooms and fry for another 5 minutes. Stir in the tomatoes and crème fraîche or cream and simmer for 5–10 minutes until reduced and thickened. Season and reserve. Place the remaining butter, flour and milk in a non-stick pan, heat gently and whisk together until smooth and thickened. Season generously and simmer for 2–3 minutes. Add the spinach and half the parmesan and heat through gently. Put one-third of the lasagne in the bottom of a buttered baking dish and spoon over half the chicken liver mixture then a third of the spinach sauce. Arrange another layer of lasagne on top and pour over the remaining chicken liver sauce, then another third of the spinach mixture. Top with the rest of the lasagne. Spoon over the rest of the spinach sauce to cover the lasagne. Scatter over the remaining parmesan and bake for 30–40 minutes until golden brown and the lasagne is tender.

< 96 >

CHICKEN FRICASSEE

This is a dish with a family connection with the Greek sauce, *avgolemono*, in that the dish is finished with a mixture of egg and lemon. It's different from the Greek version though in that very little runny sauce is left at the end of it, and the heat from the chicken cooks the egg, making it cling to it rather like a satiny coat.

Serves 4.

Ingredients

30 g/1 oz each olive oil and butter
100 g/4 oz onion
300 ml/½ pint of chicken stock (a cube is fine)
juice of 1½ lemons
Salt and pepper

4 chicken breasts
1 clove of garlic
1 tsp cornflour
1 egg
1 egg yolk

Method

Melt the butter in the oil and fry the chicken breasts, skin side down, until they are golden. Turn them over and cook for another 4 or 5 minutes in the fat. Add the finely chopped onion and garlic and sauté until transparent. Pour in the chicken stock and simmer, partly covered, for another 15 minutes until the chicken is cooked through and the stock almost vanished. Season generously with salt and pepper. Mix the cornflour into the lemon juice and beat the egg and egg yolk together. Mix that with the lemon juice and cornflour mixture. Turn the pan up to maximum, remove from the heat and pour in the egg and lemon juice mixture, turning the chicken in it rapidly. The idea is not to make an omelette on the bottom of the pan but to coat the chicken with the mixture. Serve immediately with a crisply fried vegetable. Zucchini with a little parmesan sprinkled over the top is ideal for this.

< 97 >

STRACOTTA

Almost everywhere in Italy there is a traditional beef stew. Sometimes it is called a *stuffato* or *stuffatno* or *spezzato* or one of a dozen names. It varies as much as the names, *stracotta* is just a local variant. Most have the same basis of beef slowly cooked to tenderness with vegetables for flavour and a variety of liquids for the sauce – red or white wines are used – stock or tomato purée also figure as does grape juice. In this version from the heart of Italy they include dried mushrooms and the famous aged vinegar of the Modena area.

Ingredients

1 kg/ 2 lb stewing beef in 2.5 cm/1 in cubes
2 cloves of garlic
30 g/1 oz dried mushrooms
50 g/2 oz concentrated tomato purée
½ tsp allspice
50 ml/2 fl oz olive oil
1 large onion
4 tbsp balsamic vinegar
1 tsp each oregano and thyme
1 bay leaf

Method

Soak the dried mushrooms in 300 ml/½ pint of hot water for 15 minutes. Sauté the meat in the oil until brown, about 5 minutes. Add the vinegar and bring to the boil for 1 minute. Peel and chop the garlic and onions, add the sauté till transparent. Remove the mushrooms saving the water and cut in quarters. Add to the stew and season. Mix the soaking water and the tomato purée together, add to the meat, put in the herbs and the allspice, bring to the boil and simmer on the stove or in a slow oven 325°F/150°C/130°C Fan/Gas Mark 3/simmering oven in an Aga, for 1½ hours. Serve with sautéd potatoes or egg pasta and sprinkle with fresh basil or parsley.

< 98 >

An Italian sweet trolley – Sicilian cheesecake p. 238; chocolate amaretti mousse p. 161; panna cotta p. 100; strawberries in balsamic vinegar p. 102; apricot ice p. 201; hot panatonne pudding p. 180; oranges in caramel p. 82

< 99 >

PANNA COTTA

This cream pudding is eaten everywhere and made in a variety of ways. Some people make it with gelatine but I prefer the more ancient traditional method that uses a flour mixture to add to the cream with an egg yolk to thicken it.

Ingredients

300 ml/½ pint of double cream

50 g/2 oz caster sugar

1 egg yolk

1 tsp vanilla essence

1 tbsp cornflour

Method

Mix the cream, the vanilla essence and the sugar together and heat in a non-stick pan until completely blended. Mix the cornflour with a little milk until it's smooth and stir in the egg yolk. Off the heat, add this mixture to the cream and stir, whisking, until blended through. Heat gently until just simmering – do not boil – and cook for about 2 minutes. Allow the mixture to cool a little and then pour it into custard cups or pretty wine glasses to cool. It improves with chilling for an hour or two.

< 100 >

TORTA DI MANDORLE

These almond cakes are a great tradition of Emilia, and are made in a variety of ways. They are eaten with coffee, as part of a more elaborate confection dressed with cream and candied fruit, or as a base for the local version of *Zuppa Inglese*, the extraordinarily named Italian trifle. A spring-sided tin is ideal for this as the cake is in some ways a slightly sticky meringue.

Ingredients

350 g/12 oz ground almonds
5 eggs, separated
Grated rind of 1 lemon

100 g/4 oz self raising flour
100 g/4 oz caster sugar
Pinch of salt

Method

Mix the flour with the ground almonds, the lemon rind and the egg yolks which have been beaten till pale yellow. In a separate bowl, whisk the egg whites with the salt until they are stiff. Add the sugar, a spoonful at a time, whisking all the while. Fold the almond mixture into the beaten whites using a metal spoon to retain as much air as possible. Pour into a greased, preferably non-stick 20 cm/8 in tin, smooth the top and bake in a medium oven, 350°F/180°C/160°C Fan/Gas Mark 4/bottom of the Aga roasting oven for about 1 hour. You may need to cover the top with a piece of greaseproof paper to stop it browning too much for the last 15 minutes. It's cooked when a skewer cones out clean. Take it out of the tin to cool thoroughly before eating. It may sink a little on cooling.

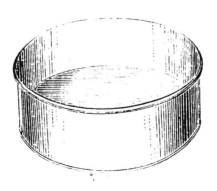

< 101 >

STRAWBERRIES IN BALSAMIC VINEGAR

An unusual flavour combination which actually works extremely well. Balsamic vinegar has a sweet richness which enhances the strawberry flavour. There is a version that leaves out the sugar and substitutes some fresh ground black pepper – I prefer the sugar!

Serves 4.

Ingredients

450 g/1 lb ripe strawberries
2 tbsp caster sugar
2 tbsp balsamic vinegar

Method

Remove the stalks from the strawberries and cut the larger berries in half. Place in a bowl and add the sugar, stirring gently to coat. Set aside for about 30 minutes or up to 1 hour until the strawberries have started to release some of their juice to make a light syrup. Sprinkle over the balsamic vinegar and stir gently to combine and leave to stand for another 10 minutes to allow the flavours to develop. Serve at room temperature in pretty, individual glass bowls. No cream!

< 102 >

TUSCANY

Tuscany, that region of Italy just above the 'knee' of the 'boot', is as much an idea as it is a place. And that's not just in the minds of foreigners from the north of Europe who, like Goethe, see Tuscany as the epitome of the fragrant south, 'the land where the lemon tree grows'. For Italians too Tuscany is in many ways the heart of their own understanding of Italy. The language that is regarded as official Italian is the Tuscan dialect. Italy's greatest poet Dante, her greatest painters and sculptors Leonardo and Michelangelo, even the best olive oil from Lucca and the most famous wine, Chianti, are all Tuscan. It's the home too of some of the most famous and beautiful cities in Italy. Florence needs little introduction but weeks to explore. At its height in the fifteenth century, ruled by the Medicis, it was the greatest city in Europe. Its wealth was the basis of that extraordinary outburst of painting, sculpture, architecture and thought that we know as the Renaissance. A stroll through the Uffizi Art Gallery takes you from the early Fra Lippi paintings through Da Vinci, Botticelli, Michelangelo, Raphael and onwards. And outside in the squares stand the legendary works of these artists (or their copies, the originals being in museums for safe keeping).

To the north and west of Florence are Lucca and Pisa, both with extraordinary medieval centres. Pisa, with its famous Leaning Tower and Cathedral, is today a great University centre. Lucca, famous for its perfect olive oil, has a wonderful central square built on the foundations of the Roman amphitheatre. Sienna to the south has its own great central square known as the Campo, where every summer they hold a traditional horse race called the Palio, with the riders all representing the City's districts or *contrade*. Surprisingly it is a genuine and local festival despite its obvious appeal for tourists.

But it is probably the Tuscan countryside that evokes images in our minds. The rolling hills, the lines of cypress bordered roads, the red-tiled villas and farmhouses tucked away in green valleys filled with vines and olive trees, fruit and corn-fields. And indeed for the Tuscans themselves this is at the very heart of their province. There are few castles in Tus-cany but many beautiful houses and mansions. The connec-tion with the countryside was and is deeply valued, and it's very much reflected in the food as well as the manners of the people. The Tuscans have a reputation for being quite severe, sober people who take their lives and their food very seriously. It was in Florence that what we would consider modern table manners first developed and the use of forks

< 103 >

Montepulciano

< 104 >

was introduced to Europe. Dante described Florence as 'sober and modest', and in the rest of Italy, at least until recently, the nickname for Tuscans was 'bean eaters' because of their love for dishes of dried white beans.

Although the area has quite a long coastline, there are no big coastal cities and fish plays a comparatively small part in the diet. Apart from the ubiquitous bean, bread is the great centre of Tuscan food, eaten in its own right, as an accompaniment to other foods, and often in dishes as well which in other parts of Italy might be eaten with pasta or rice. Meat plays an important part, with perhaps the most famous being the Florentine T-bone steaks, Costata alla Fiorentina. At their best these come from the Chianina cattle from the valley of the same name. These are huge, white-coloured animals that by the age of two years are bigger than any British domestic cow, and produce *vitellone*, a meat with the tenderness of veal but the colour and some of the flavour of beef. Game is eaten very widely, particularly hare, and there are a number of dishes in which it's used as a sauce base as well. Olives and olive oil are essential to the cuisine, and the regulation by which the oils are controlled is quite extraordinary with four levels of virgin oil alone. Mixed with onions, tomatoes and garlic it forms the basis of many sauces, ragùs, soups and salads that are at the heart of much of Tuscan cooking.

There are not many puddings in the conventional sense from Tuscany, although there are some unusual cakes, particularly one made of chestnut flour. This used to be a poor people's food but in recent years has enjoyed something of a revival, and the Castagnaccio, originally from Lucca, a thick plain cake made of chestnut flour and flavoured with pine nuts and mixed peel, is now available in bakeries all over the region and from Italian grocers all over the world. So too is the perhaps more attractive Panforte di Siena, a seasonal speciality of the town of Siena made of nuts and dried fruit in a way that must be almost identical to the medieval recipe that Dante refers to. Surprisingly it's quite easy to make at home. What isn't so easy however is the other great speciality of the region, ice-cream. There is a view, and it's one I find difficult to dissent from, that the best ice-cream in the world is to be found in Florence. I myself have a favourite ice-cream parlour, about the shape and size of a thirty-foot hall corridor hidden away behind the Cathedral Square. But all the ice-creams of Florence and the surrounding area are rightly famous. Once again their origins are from the East, but the modern flavours and range are quite extraordinary. Grape ice-creams are made from all the various coloured grapes, there are three or four different kinds of melon ice-creams and sorbets, and ice-creams flavoured with honey, spices and almonds and, above all, with the extraordinary fruits of the region.

Perhaps my most vivid memory of Tuscany is of my first visit to Florence, as a student, seeing the little carts in the streets selling fruits and chunks of coconut and water melon kept cool and moist by never-ending small jets of water dribbled over them. There are fewer of them these days, no doubt hygiene regulations have played a part, but there can be few pleasures to match sitting in the summer shade of one of the renaissance masterpieces of that city, with a chunk of chilled water melon and a giant, golden, fragrant peach, and watching the world go past in a city that for half a thousand years has been at the heart of Europe's civilisation.

< 105 >

Preparation at La Grotta, Radicofani

< 106 >

EATING OUT

Eating out in Tuscany is one of life's great pleasures, but don't always look for the most expensive restaurants. There is a tradition, particularly in Florence, of little trattoria where food is served at communal tables and you sit and eat in mixed company, not always of your own choosing, but usually lively and friendly. A few words of Italian will help of course, but while credit cards may not be accepted, good nature certainly will. It's probably in one of these restaurants that your chance to taste the famous Florentine beef steak should be taken, and look also for Ribollita, the literally twice-cooked bean soup with onions, olive oil and tomatoes. In the autumn it's worth looking for game dishes, particularly those made with hare. Bean dishes, some of them not obvious (salads of beans and tuna fish with an onion and lemony dressing) are specialities. Dishes made with spinach, with fish, chicken or eggs nestling in them and covered with a bechamel sauce are worth looking for. And not to be missed, when it's available, is the split grilled chicken. This is a traditional way of cooking chicken that goes back to Etruscan times. It's often quite highly spiced and ideally it's cooked over vine clippings. Chianti is the great red wine of the area. Little cheese is made in Tuscany, as the cattle tend to be bred for beef rather than for milk, except, surprisingly, for some sheep's milk cheese, pecorino, made by shepherds who have emigrated from Sardinia to the uplands of Tuscany where they keep huge flocks of sheep on pastures richer than those on their native island.

Ponte Vecchio, Florence

< **107** >

TUSCAN BEAN SOUP

This is a marvellous soup often eaten as part of lunch in the countryside. But it is full of so many goodies it's really a meal in itself. It's packed with protein and flavour, and although the list of ingredients is long, it is very easy to make. Dried beans are quite cheap, but you must soak them for 6 hours or according to the instructions on the packet, or use a tin.

Serves 4.

Ingredients

225 g/8 oz cannellini or borlotti beans (or a 450 g/1 lb can, drained)
2 bay leaves
4 tbsp olive oil
1 bunch of spring onions, chopped
225 g/8 oz carrots, diced
4 celery sticks, thinly sliced
175 g/6 oz stringless green beans, topped and tailed
350 g/12 oz green cabbage, shredded
50 g/2 oz small pasta shapes, such as macaroni
1 tbsp chopped fresh parsley
Salt and freshly ground black pepper
Freshly grated parmesan, to garnish

Method

Soak the beans for at least 6 hours, or according to the instructions on the packet, drain and rinse them well, then put them into a pan and cover with water. Add the bay leaves and olive oil, turn up the heat and boil fast for 10 minutes. Then turn the heat down and simmer for 1–1½ hours or until the beans are tender. If using a tin start here with the drained beans and olive oil. Add the spring onions, carrots, celery, green beans, cabbage and pasta and pour in 900 ml–1.2 litres/1½–2 pints of water until you have achieved the soup-like consistency. Season generously, bring to the boil and simmer for 15–20 minutes until the vegetables and pasta are tender. Stir in the parsley, ladle into soup bowls and serve with plenty of parmesan.

< 108 >

Tuscan bean soup p. 108; potato gnocchi p. 112; pansanella p. 110

< 109 >

PANSANELLA

This recipe for a very simple country salad based on bread and tomatoes, not only has a variety of different recipes depending on who you speak to, but also a variety of spellings. Either way it makes a quite extraordinary and substantial salad, as part of the tradition of the *cucina di povera* or 'poor people's cooking', that plays such an important part in Tuscan culinary tradition. It is very important to use the ripest possible tomatoes for this and the vine ripened variety that are now available in Britain seem to have much more flavour and sweetness than others and are probably best for the recipe.

Ingredients

4 slices of white bread with a firm crumb
225 g/8 oz ripe tomatoes
1 x 7.5 cm/3 in section of cucumber
2 spring onions
6 fresh basil leaves
1 clove of garlic
5 tbsp olive oil
2 tbsp red wine vinegar
Salt and pepper

Method

Put the bread into a bowl and cover with cold water. Let it absorb the water, pour the water off and then squeeze the bread dry, making sure you don't squeeze it too hard so that it becomes a kind of paste. When most of the water is out of it, flake it into a salad bowl. Peel the cucumber, scoop the seeds out from the centre with a teaspoon and chop finely. Halve the tomatoes and squeeze out any runny seeds or liquid. Chop those finely and add them. Clean and chop the spring onions and tear the basil leaves into small pieces with your fingers. Mix all the ingredients together. Season generously and pour over the wine vinegar. Crush the garlic and mix with the olive oil. Mix that into the salad as a whole and give it a couple of thorough turns and leave to stand out of the fridge for at least half an hour before eating. It is usually eaten as a first course but can be part of an *antipasti* or even a light dish for supper or lunch in its own right.

< 110 >

SPAGHETTI GAMBERETTI

Tuscany's not much of a place for fish dishes although there are the occasional specialities on the coast – a Livorenese fish stew and a dish of baby eels or elvers which comes from near Pisa. But there are restaurants that serve fish and particularly the almost universal spaghetti with prawns. The prawns used for this dish though are really rather larger than the North Atlantic ones we normally buy ready cooked and if you are hoping to cook it at home perhaps the best thing to look for is the unshelled tiger prawns that are sold raw in the frozen food cabinet of most of our supermarkets. Shelling them is a bit fiddly in the middle of the dish but the benefit of the flavour starting with raw prawns is quite extraordinary. Serve this in bowls with a spoon and fork to eat it with. It's traditional to eat it as only part of a main meal but in these days of lighter eating you may find that with a little starter and some cheese or fruit it's sufficient for most appetites.

Ingredients

4 ripe tomatoes (or half a tin of Italian tomatoes)
450 g/1 lb raw headless prawns, shell on
2 sticks of celery with the leaves
1 tsp dried basil
2 tbsp olive oil

1 onion
2 carrots
½ tsp chilli powder
1 tbsp chopped parsley
450 g/1 lb fine spaghetti

1 clove of garlic

Method

Put the prawns into 300 ml/½ pint of boiling salted water until they turn bright red. Take them out, reserving the water, and shell them. Chop the carrot, celery and onion together, add that to the water, salt, bring to the boil and simmer for 30 minutes. In a separate pan, put the oil and the finely chopped garlic and let it go golden. Add the tomatoes, chopped if they are whole, and the chilli powder. Add a cup of the strained stock and simmer for 20 minutes. Cook the spaghetti in boiling, salted water with a drop of oil in it until it's just tender, about 7–8 minutes, and drain. Add the prawns to the hot sauce, check the seasoning and stir in the chopped and dried herbs. Divide the spaghetti into 4 bowls and pour the sauce over it. It's not usual to use parmesan cheese with this dish.

< 111 >

POTATO GNOCCHI

Although pasta is eaten all over Italy, in Tuscany it's not a central part of the cuisine. There are one or two eccentrically shaped pastas eaten with game dishes, but what is local are the gnocchi – little dumplings made of potatoes and sometimes other bases like pumpkin, eaten with the same sort of sauces you might eat with pasta. They are quite simple to make and even, nowadays, available ready-made at the fresh pasta counters of supermarkets. But the flavour from a simple one of your own made at home is quite remarkably different from anything you can buy from a shop. Unlike home-made pasta in its proper form, these are also very easy to make and handle.

Ingredients

900 g/2 lb potatoes
225 g/8 oz bread flour (unbleached white)
1 tsp salt
1 egg yolk

For the sauce
175 g/6 oz gorgonzola
150 ml/5 fl oz (1 carton) double cream
1 tbsp butter
Fresh grated parmesan

Method

Do not cut the potatoes although you should trim and scrub them thoroughly. Put them to boil in their skins. Some recipes require you to steam them but I find this makes little difference. When they are tender, remove from the water and let them drain in a colander for at least 5 minutes. Split them and scoop out the floury centres into a warm bowl. Mash the potatoes, add the egg yolk, and then mix into them, tablespoon by tablespoon, the white flour. Depending on how moist the potatoes are you may need a little less or even a little more flour. The idea is to make the dough using as little flour as will help it stick together. It should be a firm dough, dry to the touch, but as soft as possible. Once the dough is made, knead it by hand for 2 or 3 minutes until it is firm and slightly springy. Divide it into 5 or 6 pieces and roll each section out into a sausage about 1 cm/½ in in diameter. Cut 1.5 cm/¾ in long lengths and, using your thumb, press a dent in the centre of each one so that it becomes like a

< 112 >

little squashed boat shape. You may need to add a little flour as you undertake the rolling and squashing process, but it is extremely therapeutic. Drop the gnocchi when they are made into a big pan of boiling salted water. Let them cook until they float to the top. As they float to the top they are cooked, and you remove them and place them into a colander. Put them into a buttered dish and, in a separate pan, mix the butter, grated cheese and cream together until it forms a smooth sauce. Season it with pepper, pour it over the gnocchi, sprinkle with a little parmesan and put under a grill for just 2–3 minutes. A delicious first course. (The gnocchi can also be eaten with the sort of tomato sauce you would eat with pasta, with or without meat.)

TURKEY SCALOPPINI

This dish is normally made from veal, but allowing for many people's sensitivities I've used turkey, which is similar in texture. Do use veal if you fancy it. You can buy the turkey breast fillets for this dish in every supermarket or you may even be able to buy ready-prepared scaloppini.

Serves 4.

Ingredients

450 g/1 lb turkey breast fillets
1 tbsp sunflower oil plus a little extra
1 tbsp chopped fresh sage

25 g/1 oz butter
250 ml/8fl oz double cream
Fresh green salad, to serve

120 ml/4 fl oz water (in parts of Tuscany they use vermouth)
350 g/12 oz fresh mixed green and white tagliatelle

Method

Put the tagliatelle in a pan of boiling salted water, add a drop of oil and cook for 5–6 minutes until just tender or according to the instructions on the packet. Drain and toss in the butter. Arrange in a large oval serving dish and keep warm. Cut the turkey breast fillets across the grain at an angle so that you have a number of mini steaks, each about 5 cm/2 in x 3 cm/1½ in. If they are very thick you may want to flatten them slightly under a sheet of greaseproof with the back of a frying pan or a meat mallet

< 113 >

until they are 5 mm/¼ in thick. Put the tablespoon of oil and the remaining butter into a large frying pan into which all the turkey will fit in one layer. Heat until the butter stops sizzling and add the scaloppini. Let them cook for 45 seconds to 1 minute on one side. Turn over and cook for another 1–1½ minutes. They should be light gold on the outside but not cooked to a dryness. Sprinkle over the sage, season generously and add the water, scraping up the bits in the bottom of the pan. Put the scaloppini on top of the tagliatelle. Stir the double cream into the pan and bring to the boil. Simmer for 2–3 minutes until the sauce amalgamates and goes pale gold. Pour the sauce over the scaloppini and serve immediately on the tagliatelle with the salad.

CHICKEN FLORENTINE

Spinach and Florence always go together in culinary terms. I remember being served it on my very first visit so maybe it's correct. This is a marvellous dish for making a little go a deliciously long way. The addition of spinach and beautiful baked cheese sauce stretches a small amount of chicken into a substantial meal for four. Use fresh spinach if you can – the pre-prepared packs of spinach make this very quick.

Serves 4.

Ingredients

4 chicken breast fillets
1 small onion, quartered
½ tsp freshly grated nutmeg
100 g/4 oz Gruyère or Cheddar cheese
Salt and freshly ground black pepper
450 g/1 lb fresh spinach or 225 g/8 oz frozen leaf spinach

1 bay leaf
300 ml/½ pint milk
25 g/1 oz plain flour
50 g/2 oz butter
Tagliatelle, to serve

Method

Preheat the oven to 375°F/190°C/170°C Fan/Gas Mark 5/middle of the Aga roasting oven. Place the chicken in a pan with the bay leaf, onion and a little salt. Pour in 300 ml/½ pint of water and bring to the boil, then immediately turn down the heat and simmer very gently for about 20 minutes. Drain. Meanwhile, whisk together the milk,

< 114 >

Chicken Florentine p. 114

< 115 >

flour and half of the butter in a non-stick pan over a medium heat to make the white sauce. Season to taste and whisk the sauce three or four times as it is coming to the boil until thick and glossy. If using fresh spinach, rinse well and plunge it or the frozen spinach into a pan of boiling water for a couple of minutes. Drain well. Melt the remaining butter and toss the spinach in it. Arrange in the bottom of an ovenproof dish. Cut the chicken into nuggets and put on top of the spinach. Mix 75 g/3 oz of the cheese and the nutmeg into the sauce and pour over the chicken. Sprinkle with the remaining cheese and bake for 15 minutes until golden and bubbling. Serve at once with pasta.

CARROTS IN MILK

Italian vegetable dishes are often unexpected and unusual, none more so than this version of carrots cooked in milk. I suspect this is an ancient tradition, and certainly the method of saucing the carrots comes from the medieval tradition of using eggs rather than flour. This is a dish quite good enough to be eaten on its own as a course, if you wish, but is also nice with the roasted or grilled meats that are so popular in Tuscany.

Ingredients

675 g/1½ lb carrots
⅓ pint (7 fl oz) milk

Salt and pepper

25 g/1 oz butter
1 egg yolk

Method

Peel the carrots and cut them into rounds about 1 cm/½ in thick. Put them into a saucepan of cold water with some salt, bring them to the boil and cook for just 3–4 minutes. Drain them and wipe out the pan. Put the butter and all but 2 or 3 tablespoons of the milk into the pan, add the carrots and simmer very gently for another 6 or 7 minutes until they are just cooked. Season generously. Mix the remaining milk with the egg yolk. Remove from the heat and stir the egg and milk mixture into the sauce in the pan to allow the heat from the vegetables and the pan itself to thicken it. As soon as it starts to thicken, transfer to a warm serving dish and serve sprinkled with parsley.

< 116 >

FAGIOLI ALL' UCCELLETTO

This is the classic dish of Tuscan baked beans. The beans themselves are almost always cannellini, the white beans similar to but not the same as the French haricot. In Tuscany they are sometimes eaten fresh, but they are very difficult to obtain like that outside of the region. Haricot beans will do as well but, either way, buy 'fresh' new seasons beans even though they are dried as, if they are kept in store for a long time, it makes them very difficult to cook well. This method of cooking the beans literally means 'in the manner of little birds' – the reason for the name seems to be lost in the mists of time, unless they were beans cooked to be eaten with the small game birds that the Italians are so fond of. In fact there's no meat in the recipe at all, even if beans cooked like this, and in the other classic Tuscan way '*a fiasco*', are marvellous eaten with grilled meat and sausages. I give here the full recipe starting with the dried beans but it is also possible to buy both borlotti and cannellini beans tinned, and you can begin the recipe half way through after the beans have been given their first cooking, if you wish, to short-cut the process.

Ingredients

450 g/1 lb dried white beans or 2 x 450 g/1 lb tins
1 tin chopped tomatoes in tomato juice
1 dessertspoon tomato purée

4 tbsp olive oil
2 cloves of garlic
Sprig of fresh sage leaves

Salt and pepper

Method

Put the dry beans into a saucepan and cover with twice their own depth of water. Soak for at least 6 hours, though 12 to 18 is better. Change the water, covering the beans again to 2.5 cm/1 in over their own depth. Do not add the salt yet. Bring the beans to the boil and simmer for 1–1½ hours until they are cooked through but have not disintegrated. This can be done in a slow oven or one of the simmering ovens of an Aga. When the beans are cooked drain them but keep some of the liquid aside. Put the oil into a clean saucepan. Crush the garlic with a knife or the heel of your hand and add that and the sage leaves and heat gently for 3 or 4 minutes without allowing the garlic or the sage to brown. Add the beans and a generous seasoning of salt and black pepper and the tomatoes. Mix together. If the mixture is still quite dry add a little of the cooking water from the beans. Bring to the boil. Cover and allow to simmer over the lowest possible heat (or in a slow oven) for ½–1 hour. The dish is very satisfactory reheated. Serve with a sprinkling of fresh sage or parsley.

< 117 >

STEAK FLORENTINE

The proper steak for this is probably not available in England because the cattle from which it comes are much larger than those we are used to and the T-bone cut will probably weigh the best part of 775 g/1¾ lb. Despite popular legend these days it will feed more than one person at that size. A good, well-hung T-bone steak is essential, because the method of cooking is extremely simple. It's traditionally done over a charcoal or wood fire but it works perfectly well under a properly pre-heated grill. I'd advise you to line the pan of the grill with foil because this not only makes the washing up easier but helps reflect back some of the heat to produce the intensity that's desirable. Everything else needs to be ready beforehand, warm plates, the table laid and something to mop up the juices. In Florence they often just use some of the wonderful bread but sauté potatoes are acceptable as well. Save any vegetables for a separate course. The Florentines always eat this dish slightly pink in the middle. If you like your meat better done, you may not want to bother because, cooked in this manner till it's brown all the way through, it will inevitably be rather dry.

Serves 4.

Ingredients

2 x 450 g–675 g/1–1½ lb T-bone steaks
2 tbsp olive oil (rosemary flavoured oil is perfect)
1 tsp salt   **Black pepper**   **1 lemon**

Method

Pre-heat the grill (or the barbecue) until it's at maximum heat. Brush the steaks with the oil but do not season them at this stage. The steaks should be about 1in thick. If they're thinner or thicker you will have to adjust the cooking times accordingly. Place on or under the hot grill for 3 minutes a side to have them very pink or 4 minutes to have them just rosy. Remove from the heat, spread with a little more oil, season generously with the salt and pepper and serve with a quarter of a piece of lemon to squeeze over the steak. If you're dividing a steak between two, you may want to divide both sides of the bone in half so that you get both a piece of the fillet and the contra fillet for each person. Serve immediately on warm plates.

< 118 >

HERBED BAKED POTATOES

The combination of rosemary and garlic is one that's very popular in Tuscany and it's used with both meats and other dishes too. This is a very simple way of producing a kind of baked herbed potato using that combination. In a way it's rather like an Italian version of British roast potatoes but with quite a different slant.

Ingredients

900 g/2 lb new or Cyprus type potatoes
2 sprigs of rosemary

3 cloves of garlic
180 ml/6 fl oz olive oil

Salt and pepper

Method

Scrub the potatoes and make sure they're cut to an even size. Put them into cold water, bring to the boil and cook for just 5 minutes. Crush the garlic but don't peel it and add it to the oil and the rosemary sprigs in a roasting pan. Put this in the oven until it's hot and, when it is, drain the potatoes thoroughly and roll them in the oil before returning to a hot oven, 400°F/200°C/180°C Fan/Gas Mark 6 or the middle of the roasting oven in the Aga, for 40–45 minutes until the potatoes are browning and cooked through. Turn them in the oil a couple of times and discard the rosemary and garlic when serving. They should not be salted until after they've finished cooking.

Baffi

< 119 >

ZUPPA INGLESE

Why this is called English soup is anyone's guess, perhaps a visitor to Britain was served trifle at the start of a meal. Anyway, it's a well established and much loved dish in the north of Italy. The traditional way of making this recipe uses crème patissière but fresh pouring custard tastes just as good and saves a lot of time.

Serves 4.

Ingredients

175 g/6 oz good quality sponge cake, such as Madeira

5 tbsp fresh orange juice

200 g/7 oz can peaches in natural juice (or fresh peaches peeled and lightly poached)

25 g/1 oz toasted almond flakes

100 g/4 oz apricot conserve or jam

350 ml/12 fl oz fresh pouring custard (made with eggs and milk)

Handful of crystallized cherries

150 ml/¼ pint whipping or double cream

Method

Place the sponge cake in a shallow dish and soak in the orange juice. Then break it up into walnut sized chunks and place in the bottom of an attractive glass bowl. Spoon over the conserve or jam. Place the peaches with their juice in a food processor or liquidizer and blend to a smooth purée. Spoon the purée over the cake and jam mixture. Whip the cream until it just holds its shape and then fold into the custard. Spread over the peach purée to cover completely. Scatter over the almonds, arrange the cherries on top and chill for at least 2 hours. Serve straight from the fridge.

< 120 >

GELATA AL LIMONE

There are literally thousands of recipes for ice-cream in Italy, ranging from the simplest granitas, which are just frozen fruit syrups, through to the confections of the south where different layers of ice-cream and nuts and fruits are mixed together. This is a very simple lemon flavoured cream, an ice-cream really for making at home, rather than one of the more varied and extraordinary confections of the ice-cream parlours of Florence and the rest of Tuscany. It catches, however, the luxury and lusciousness of those fabulous emporia of delight.

Ingredients

2 lemons

75 g/3 oz caster sugar

150 ml/¼ pint double cream

4 egg yolks

450 ml/¾ pint milk

Pinch of salt

½ tsp vanilla essence (real vanilla if possible)

Method

Beat the yolks with the sugar and the salt until they reach what's known as the 'ribbon' stage. This means they go lemon yellow and can leave a trail when you move the beater through them. I find an electric beater does this job better than most things. Heat the milk and cream with the grated rind of both lemons until just below the boiling point. Take it off the heat and allow it to cool for 5 minutes. Add it, a spoonful at a time, to the egg mixture in the bowl, and then place the bowl in a saucepan of boiling water (or use the top of a double boiler if you prefer), and stir gently until the mixture thoroughly coats the back of a spoon. Under no circumstances allow it to come near to boiling point, or you will wind up with complicated scrambled egg. When it has thickened allow it to cool and then, if you have an ice-cream making machine place it in that and chill until the ice-cream is made. If you do not, put it into a plastic container and place it in the freezer for 2–3 hours. Remove from the freezer and put into a food processor and process until mixed thoroughly and reasonably smooth. Place back in the container and freeze again for another 1½ hours or so. Either way, if you've stored the ice-cream in the freezer after making it, put it into the fridge for ½ hour to soften slightly before serving.

< 121 >

PANFORTE DI SIENA

I was first given this delicious sweetmeat to eat by some Italian neighbours more than 20 years ago. They didn't come from Siena themselves, but regarded it as the great Christmas treat. I was astonished at its taste and texture. It somehow seemed to have the richness and complexity of medieval tapestry and, indeed, it is at least as ancient as that in tradition, supposedly having come in its original form from the Middle East, brought back by traders dealing in dried fruits and spices. It's surprisingly easy to make at home though the ingredients are quite rich. This recipe was helped much by Jane Grigson's experiments in the field some years ago.

Ingredients

100 g/4 oz each of hazelnuts, almonds, candied orange, lemon and citron peel
(you can substitute 350 g/12 oz mixed peel for this)
100 g/4 oz crystallized cherries
100 g/4 oz caster sugar
2 tsp cinnamon
100 g/4 oz chopped angelica
100 g/4 oz flour
4 tbsp runny honey
½ tsp mixed spice

Method

Mix all the ingredients, except the honey and sugar, together. Put the honey and sugar in a non-stick pan and heat gently until just below boiling. Mix with the dry ingredients. Line two 20 cm/8 in loose-bottomed cake or flan tins with rice paper (this is an edible paper that acts both as a container and an insulator). Pour the mixture equally into the tins, smooth down and cover with another sheet of rice paper. Bake in a low oven, 300°F/160°C/150°C Fan/Gas Mark 2, the top of a simmering oven in the Aga, for 35–40 minutes. Allow to cool before removing from the tins. It can be stored in an airtight container for 3 to 4 months comfortably. To serve, cut in fairly small triangular slices. This is a surprisingly rich cake and a little goes a long way.

< 122 >

The sweet life in Tuscany – Gelata al limone p. 121; panforte di Siena p. 122

< 123 >

Wildflowers, Umbria

< 124 >

UMBRIA & THE MARCHES

Umbria is Italy's inland and private province. At no point does it get within one hundred kilometres of the sea. It straddles the mountain chain of the Apennines to the north of Rome and boasts none of the great cities of modern Italy. The Marches, which run from its borders down to the Adriatic Sea, are even more remote and, possibly with the exception of one or two areas of the south, the least well-known and least populated part of Italy. The two towns, or cities to give them their proper dignity, which are the centres of the two sister provinces, are Perugia in Umbria and Urbino in the Marches. Perugia began its life as one of the great towns of the Etruscans five hundred years before Christ; later, its proximity to Rome and the Papal states led the whole region into a series of conflicts with Papal authority which resulted in Church rule for the last three hundred years before the independence of Italy. There are some strange legacies from that time: one of the most hated aspects of the Papal hegemony was a salt tax and to this day in Perugia they bake their bread without salt as an historic protest. There is a sense of spirituality in the area, encouraged it must be said these days by the tourist trade, which is unique in the Italy of bustling cathedral squares where church business means the stock exchange as much as the Bishop's Palace. They say that twenty thousand saints have been born in Umbria. The cynical might believe that's because they were close enough to Rome for their miracles to be recognized, but even the most cynical recognize the extraordinary influence of such people as St Francis of Assisi, the kindly saint who stood for the welfare of animals and birds as much as for humans.

Although Perugia is the capital of Umbria and has wonderful buildings, traditions and a superb fountain to remind you of the fact, it's Assisi that is its spiritual heart. It's an almost picture postcard town of grey pink stone houses under tile roofs straggling up the hill from the great Basilica of St Francis towards 'the great rock', the Rocca Maggiore – the remains of fortifications that glower down from the hill above the town. The other great saint of Umbria, St Benedict, came from Norcia, today the centre of truffles and salami. Umbria still has a reputation for the arts in modern times, and Spoletto is renowned for its festival of two worlds specializing in modern art of all sorts, but in food terms the region remains perhaps the most traditional of all of Italy. Even approaching the coast the country is dramatic and often falls precipitously into the sea. Along the coast though there are a number of beaches and of course the traditional range of coastal fisherman's cafés, tavernas, stews and soups. Even here the Marches manage to maintain an individuality with a range of

< 125 >

dishes cooked almost defiantly without tomatoes, *a bianco* it's called, fish flavoured with wine vinegar and herbs rather than the chillies and tomatoes from further down the coast.

What Umbria and the Marches share, apart from their isolation and hills, is the truffle, the great prized underground mushroom that in its rarer manifestations is literally worth its weight in gold; quite ordinary truffles sell currently for over £400 a kilo. The truffles of the mountains tend to be black, or at least grey, and brown rather than white like the truffles of Alba. Umbria by and large produces black ones. In the season there are great markets and festivals held for these prized fungi. They are at times so common that the locals eat them with everything, in sauces with spaghetti, with eggs, in omelettes, frittata and scrambled eggs; they're served with cheese, and even chopped up and used as a garnish for grilled meat. They're mixed with the famous olives of the region and turned into spreads that are eaten on toasted bread, and they're preserved and tinned and canned as well. They work quite well frozen, but preserved truffles are probably best avoided, particularly as they show no signs of reflecting their weak flavour in their price. You can occasionally find them in Britain (indeed Britain produces black truffles, though they are little harvested and not much known). The trick is to buy one and use it in one of the dishes that spreads its flavour best. Eggs, cheese and cream are usually the best carriers. An alternative is to buy one of the truffled olive oils that have made their appearance on the market. These are also formidably expensive, but the best ones carry a real sense of the truffle and can be used to brush grilled meats, to pour into a mushroom soup, or to cook a dish of eggs with, providing the authentic flavour. The oil that the truffles are usually steeped in is another local speciality. It's produced in small quantities on the steep hillsides, but it's very highly regarded and very highly flavoured, being the most spicy of all the Italian olive oils. The olives themselves are much used, particularly in black form in Umbria and green in the Marches. The olives of Ascoli are amazingly large, so big that they are stoned, stuffed and deep fried as a delicacy in their own right. Preserved meats are another famous product of the area, particularly of the south east around Norcia, where salamis and hams of all sorts are supposed to be the best in Italy. Indeed, the word for a pork butcher over most of Italy is *norcino*, naming the skill after the town which has become famous for it.

In an area where the climate has so much to do with the food, game is an important part of the diet, and indeed almost anything that moves is shot in the season, an anomaly near the birthplace of St Francis. All kinds of game are eaten, from the little birds on migratory passage in season through to rabbit and hare. These are often cooked in quite rich sauces or in the local herbs in an almost dry manner whereby the flavour of the

< 126 >

herbs gets impregnated into the meat. Lentils are used extensively, both with the sausages and stews of the region, and also with game; although the production isn't large, the lentils from Castelluccio have a wonderful reputation.

Grilling is one of the favourite ways of cooking with fish on the coast, meat in the mountains and game, chicken and rabbit in the towns. Lamb is a favourite meat, particularly in the area of the border between Umbria and the Marches where great herds of sheep are kept, mainly for their milk for cheese. Pecorino from the area is widely admired whether it's made in its natural form, perfumed with local herbs, or wrapped in chestnut leaves. There's not much fish eaten except near the coast of the Marches, though there is some freshwater fish, particularly trout and mullet from the area around Lake Trasimeno. It is usually grilled, as fish is sufficiently rare not to require much fancy cooking.

Although there are no formal puddings, there is a huge range of what we would think of as biscuits, and firm cakes made to be dipped in wine or coffee or even, if the mood takes you, a herb tea. Dunking is a great habit here, they dunk bread in wine as well as the sweeter specialities with wonderful names like Tozzetti and Ciambelloni. While claims are made all over the world for various ancient cooking traditions, the pattern of eating and cooking in Umbria and the high Marches has such a feeling of ancientness about it that it's here, more than anywhere else I know, that that claim seems to have some ring of truth about it.

Perugia

< 127 >

EATING OUT

Lacking any great cosmopolitan towns, the area tends to specialize in small local restaurants, serving local food to local people. Outsiders or foreigners are always made welcome if they comport themselves properly. The people of Umbria are notorious for being the most traditional and 'old fashioned' in their manners and opinions of any in Italy, and it's often wise to ask the opinion of the owner or manager (usually the same person) of the restaurant as to the local specialities of the time of year and those foods that don't appear on the menu.

Perugia, the main town of the area, is astonishingly small and therefore often seems crowded, with students rather than with tourists, although there is plenty to see, particularly the works of some of the local artists: Francesco da Rimini, fra Angelico and Piero della Francesca to mention but a few. It's a big student town and therefore, in addition to the one or two grander restaurants based around the hotels, there are lots and lots of student eating places: cafés, a few pizza and pasta centres, but also some old fashioned trattoria where the students and the townspeople mix, sometimes, it must be said, a little uneasily. When it hasn't got its festival on in the summer, Spoletto is like a slightly smaller version of Perugia. Assisi and to a lesser extent Gubbio suffer from the culinary blight that mass tourism brings. Assisi is about the only place in Umbria that's full of tourists most of the time, but you really have to get out of the town a little bit to some of the smaller villages (where some of the most interesting of the various saints' relics and memorials are to be found) to find real local cooking. Always expect the specialities of the region to be the best things to order: truffles in the truffle season, try them in all the various ways that they can be had or recommended, they're often not listed on the menu. Chestnuts, and other mushrooms are also a speciality of the autumn. Around Norcia sausage-based dishes are almost inevitable, though lighter dishes cooked with truffles are well known as well. There are some specialities that make use of the local oil. Salads of lightly cooked vegetables dressed in the oil with just a hint of lemon and some herbs to make a mild and delicate dish full of health and flavour. Near Lake Trasimeno the freshwater fish is a speciality though, as that lake has become more and more a holiday playground, you may find it fairly scarce, or at least significantly expensive in the summer.

Urbino, in the Marches, is perhaps the least spoilt of all the hilltop towns of Italy, with an incredible set of late Renaissance buildings and defences still intact. Gastronomically though it doesn't have quite the same impact. The food's simple, very seasonal and by many Italian standards quite plain, though the raw materials, including the ubiquitous truffles, are often quite spectacular in their own right. One of the great things about Urbino and the area around it is that they eat the food they grow themselves and so a local dish has a double meaning. Down by the coast you'll be eating fish in one of the many ways they cook it locally, in the distinctive Marches style, very often using vinegar and herbs, lemon juice and olives rather than some of the more common ingredients found in fish cookery across the rest of Italy.

< 128 >

This is a country of little inns in little villages often frequented only by the locals where a smile and the seeking of advice can often produce a rustic meal of real pleasure and enthusiasm. In the bigger towns do look for the speciality bakers who produce a different cake for each season. Biscuits with pine nuts at Christmas, brioches at Easter and on Saints Days, often enriched with unusual and extraordinary flavours. In the towns around Assisi they make a kind of fig roll spiked with all kinds of unexpected ingredients such as bananas, crystallized orange peel, almonds and prunes, which once again local tradition has it, goes back to the time of the Frankish knights who came here in medieval times. As with so much in Umbria and the Marches, it's food with simple but strong flavours and an intense local tradition that gives the most pleasure in restaurants or in one of the many shops when buying for your mountainside picnic.

Shopping in Norcia

< 129 >

Hot zucchini salad p. 131; crostini p. 131

< 130 >

CROSTINI

All over Italy there are various kinds of baked breads or toasts spread with an equally great variety of toppings. In Umbria these tend to be based on olives and to resemble very much the Provençal tapenade that, like its Umbrian relation, could well go back to a classical Roman tradition of olive and anchovy pastes. You can make this paste in advance and store it in the fridge under a little olive oil and cling film for up to a fortnight. It's pretty strongly flavoured and a little goes quite a long way.

Ingredients

225 g/8 oz black olives, pitted (stone removed)
30 g/1 oz capers (removed from their
   vinegar and rinsed)
100 ml/4 fl oz olive oil

1 tin anchovies in oil
1 clove of garlic
Grated rind of 1 orange

Method

You can do this by hand with a pestle and mortar but much the simplest way is to place all the ingredients together in a food processor and process for about 10–15 seconds. Scrape the sides down and process again for about 4 or 5 seconds. The mixture should be fairly smooth but should contain some texture. Put it into small earthenware or ceramic pots and keep it in the fridge. To use, spread it quite thinly (not quite as thinly as marmite but only just) on slices of good bread that have been toasted in the oven or under the grill until light gold. Serve immediately with plenty to drink as the flavour is intense and salty.

HOT ZUCCHINI SALAD

This is a very simple salad with unusual ingredients, not least because the courgettes are served hot. It's flavoured with mountain herbs and takes only a moment or two to make, especially if you keep a jar of well made olive oil vinaigrette dressing in the fridge (to achieve this make four times the quantity and keep it in a sealed jar in the fridge to use at your discretion).

< 131 >

Ingredients

450 g/1 lb small shiny courgettes
2 tbsp olive oil
1 clove of garlic
1 tbsp fresh oregano (or marjoram)
1 pinch thyme leaves (fresh if possible)

For the dressing

½ tsp each sugar and salt   4 tbsp red wine vinegar
8 tbsp olive oil   Splash of lemon juice

Method

Cut the ends off the courgettes and then cut them into 5 mm/¼ in rounds. Sauté these rapidly in a frying pan with the finely chopped clove of garlic in 2 tablespoons of olive oil. They should cook till they're pale gold, flecked on both sides. It takes about 10 minutes. Meanwhile, put the sugar and salt into the vinegar in a jar and cap and shake until the sugar and salt have dissolved. Add the oil and the splash of lemon juice and shake thoroughly again. You can do this in a liquidizer which will completely homogenize the dressing into a thick and creamy sauce. When the courgettes are cooked, tip them out of the pan onto a sheet of kitchen paper to absorb any spare cooking oil. Place them in an attractive dish in a layer not more than 1 cm/½ in deep. Pour some of the dressing over them, turn thoroughly, add the herbs and allow to stand for 5 minutes before serving. A little more dressing may be helpful as the hot courgettes will absorb most of the first dose. Crusty bread, wholemeal or white, is perfect for soaking up the delicious juices.

FISH SOUP 'BIANCO'

Each of the fishing villages and ports around the Italian coast have their own version of fish soup or stew, and the fishermen of the Marches are not an exception. On this East coast however, the soups often have a little vinegar added and are cooked 'bianco' that is without the tomato that is everywhere in the South. The mixture of fish depends on the day's catch, but try to find at least two varieties and some shell fish. And ask for the trimmings, most fish counters and shops will be glad to give you plenty.

< 132 >

Fish soup bianco p. 132

< 133 >

Ingredients

225 g/8 oz firm white fish (huss, haddock or bream, etc.)

225 g/8 oz red fish (red mullet, gurnard or tilapia)

225 g/8 oz shell fish (mussels, raw prawns or squid)

450 g/1 lb fish trimmings

50 ml/2 fl oz white wine vinegar

Handful chopped parsley

1 lemon

1 bay leaf

Parsley stalks

225 g/8 oz onions

2 cloves of garlic

50 ml/2 fl oz olive oil

Method

Put the fish trimmings, the cut off ends of the lemon, the bay leaf and parsley stalks in a saucepan with 1.2 litres/ 2 pints of water. Simmer for ½ hour and strain. Peel and finely chop the onion and garlic while the stock is cooling and cook gently in the oil for 15 minutes. Clean and cut up the fish into spoon-sized pieces (you can put the discarded bits and bones in the stock pot). Add the fish pieces to the onion mixture with the vinegar, bring to the boil, season generously and pour in the hot stock. Cook until the fish flakes – not more than 5 minutes. Season and add plenty of chopped parsley and serve with crusty bread.

FRITTATA WITH TRUFFLES

Truffles are the great speciality of the Marches and Umbria. They are so common there that they are used in all sorts of dishes. In Britain, where they cost their weight in gold, we have to be more sparing. Eggs go well with them as in this flat omelette. Do use fresh truffles – it's not worth cooking with anything else. Antonio Carluccio's shop in Neal Street in London often has them and does mail order.

Serves 4.

Ingredients

175 g/6 oz potatoes, sliced

1 tbsp freshly grated parmesan

Salt and freshly ground black pepper

2 tbsp olive oil

50 g/2 oz onions, sliced

4 eggs

Truffle shavings (15 g/½ oz minimum)

< 134 >

Method

Boil the potatoes in a pan of boiling salted water for about 5 minutes until nearly tender. Drain. Heat the oil in a 20 cm/8 in frying pan and gently fry the onions until they are just beginning to turn golden. Add the sliced potatoes and stir to combine. Leave to cook for a minute while you beat the eggs until just frothy, season well, stir in the truffles and add to the pan. Mix together gently and cook over a medium to high heat for 2–3 minutes. The egg should now be firm and everything else hot through. Sprinkle over the parmesan and place the pan under a hot grill for 1–2 minutes until the top of the omelette is brown and bubbly.

PLAICE FRITTERS WITH PARMESAN

Although plaice has a very delicate flavour, it combines very well with the robustness of parmesan. This is a very quick dish to cook, first on top of the stove and then finished off under the grill. Have all your vegetables ready so the fish doesn't have time to hang around! Other flat fish such as sole or brill make a good alternative.

Serves 4.

Ingredients

4 x 175 g/6 oz plaice fillets, cut into 5 cm/2 in strips

30 g//1 oz butter	1 tbsp sunflower oil
2 tbsp freshly grated parmesan	1 tbsp chopped fresh parsley
½ tsp garlic salt	Fresh green salad, to serve

Method

Turn on the grill to maximum. In a frying pan, large enough to hold the fillet pieces in one layer, heat the butter in the oil until it stops sizzling. Put the plaice strips, skin-side up, and sauté for just one minute. Turn the fillets over so the skin-side is down and sauté for another 1–2 minutes until just cooked through. Sprinkle with the parmesan, parsley and garlic salt, covering as much of the fish as possible. Put the pan under the grill, which should by now be really hot, for just 1 minute, to allow the parmesan to colour. Serve immediately, pouring any pan juices over the fish.

< 135 >

SAUSAGES WITH LENTILS

The sausages for this dish will almost certainly, in Umbria and the Marches, be the fennel flavoured pork sausages that are so common there, but impossible to find except in one or two Italian delicatessens in Britain. I personally favour the coarse cut beef sausages often made with Aberdeen Angus beef that a number of our better supermarket chains have begun selling recently, but you may have a local butcher who will make you good, coarse cut, meat rich sausages. Traditionally, this dish is cooked with the lentils and the sausages kept separate, until they arrive on the plate. I think that putting them together for a little while beforehand improves the flavour and texture of both.

Ingredients

675 g/1½ lb good, meaty, coarse ground sausages
1 tsp fennel seeds (optional)
4 plum or similar tomatoes
2 tbsp olive oil

4 stalks of celery
225 g/8 oz onions
2 carrots
Salt and pepper

225 g/8 oz green or brown lentils (the red ones won't do for this)

Method

Soak the lentils in plenty of water for at least 1 hour and up to 6 hours. Throw the water away. In a pan which will take all the lentil ingredients and the sausages in due course, put the olive oil and fry gently the cleaned and chopped onion, celery, and carrot. Add the lentils. Cover with water to a depth of 2.5 cm/1 in above and bring to the boil. Simmer gently for about half an hour until the lentils are cooked and almost all the water is absorbed. You may need to add a little more depending on the individual lentils you're using. Chop up the tomatoes and add those to the lentil mixture, seasoning generously at this point. Fry the sausages, either in their own fat or in a little extra oil, until they are well browned. Add them and the fennel seeds, if you are using them, to the lentil mixture, making sure that the mixture is still quite runny and moist. Cook with the lid on and the sausages at least partly buried for another 15 minutes over a very low heat for the flavours to blend. Serve each person their sausages and lentils in a deep plate. The lentils should still be, while not soupy, quite moist and runny. No other vegetable is needed at this point.

< 136 >

MACCHERONI STRASCINATI

Despite its unusual name, which is supposed to mean dragged maccheroni, this is a recipe that in technique is quite similar to the Roman favourite of Pasta Carbonara. The heat from the cooked pasta is used to set an egg-based sauce. However, this is a rather more robust dish as it uses, traditionally, the sausagemeat from the famous Umbrian sausages. You can use sausagemeat as well though ours tends to be a lot less exciting and well flavoured than theirs. You might want to try as an alternative some minced chicken or turkey flavoured with a teaspoon of fennel seeds, which seem to be an essential ingredient in this dish.

Ingredients

275 g/10 oz short cut macaroni   1 tbsp each of oil and butter
450 g/1 lb sausagemeat or minced meat mixed with 1 tsp fennel seeds
225 ml/ 8 fl oz chicken stock (a cube is fine)

For the sauce:

2 eggs   1 tbsp milk
100 g/4 oz parmesan, grated   Good pinch of salt and pepper

Method

Put the macaroni to cook in plenty of boiling salted water for about 3 minutes. Take it off the heat, put the lid on and leave it to stand. Meanwhile, heat the butter in the oil until it's completely melted. Add the sausagemeat or minced meat and the fennel seeds and fry gently for about 6 or 7 minutes. Drain the pasta, add that to the meat and pour in the broth. Simmer very gently for another 5–6 minutes until the pasta and meat are completely cooked. In a bowl whisk the eggs together with the milk, the salt and half the cheese. Pour this into the meat and pasta mixture over the lowest possible heat and stir gently with a wooden spoon, drawing the egg mixture through the pasta and meat mixture until it forms a creamy sauce. Serve in bowls with plenty of parsley sprinkled over and the rest of the cheese left for individual diners to add. This dish really needs to be served on its own as it's pretty substantial.

< 137 >

RABBIT WITH HERBS

Rabbit's a very popular meat in Italy, far more so than in Britain where it tends to be regarded as a poor relation. This method of cooking with very little liquid is used for a lot of game including pigeon, guinea fowl and, occasionally, pheasant although that's usually roasted without hanging rather as a kind of wild chicken. This used to be cooked in a parchment case, you can use foil now, but I prefer doing it in a saucepan with a really close fitting lid. A layer of foil under the lid is probably a satisfactory way of achieving this seal if your lids are a bit loose.

Ingredients

1 sprig of rosemary   2 sprigs of oregano or marjoram   2 bay leaves
**(fresh or on the branch herbs are pretty important in this dish, the dried ones
stick all over the rabbit and change the flavour considerably)**
1 rabbit, jointed   Juice and grated rind of 1 lemon
2 tbsp olive oil   1 clove of garlic

Method

Heat the oil in the bottom of a saucepan into which the pieces will all just go and sauté the rabbit for 2–3 minutes until sealed on the outside. Crush the garlic but do not remove from its wrapper. Add that and place the herbs amongst the rabbit pieces. Pour over the juice of the lemon and add the grated rind. Shake gently to mix everything together. Put on as close to an airtight lid as you can and cook over the lowest possible heat. A heat-diffusing pad is often useful in this connection. The rabbit should be cooked through in about 40 minutes and should have a very little, but intensely flavoured juice at the bottom of the pan. Season it generously with salt and pepper before serving. It's often served in the Marches with some very coarse, almost ragged, hand-made pasta, but I think it goes well with our rather more smooth-sided tagliatelle well coated with butter.

< 138 >

Rabbit with herbs p. 138

< 139 >

CHICKEN WITH
TRUFFLE FLAVOURED STUFFING

This is an occasion, if you can't find real truffles, for using truffle oil to flavour the bird. It's a stuffing technique used for all sorts of birds from the smallest to full-sized chickens. I find probably the most suitable are the poussin or spring chickens that are available everywhere in Britain. If you can't find truffles or truffle oil, try including some wild mushrooms in the recipe. If they are dried, soak them in boiling water for 15 minutes and include a little of the water in the stuffing mixture.

Ingredients

225 g/8 oz Italian style sausagemeat or minced chicken or turkey
2 large or 4 small poussin   100 g/4 oz chicken livers
50 g/2 oz fresh white breadcrumbs   1 egg
1 tbsp truffle oil   1 tbsp finely chopped parsley
Slices of truffle (optional) or 1 oz dried mushrooms
Salt and pepper

Method

Fry the minced meat or sausagemeat gently in half the truffle oil. Add the chopped chicken livers, the truffle or dried mushrooms (chopped if you are using them) and cook for about 4–5 minutes until the meat has taken colour and the liver is opaque. Put into a bowl, add the breadcrumbs, the parsley and a little liquid. If you're using dried mushrooms add a little of their liquid or a couple of tablespoonfuls of water or milk. Add the egg and mix together into a firm mixture. Season generously. Use this to stuff the poussin. Spread the remaining truffle oil over the birds and cover each one with a butter paper or piece of greaseproof paper. Roast on a rack in a roasting tin with half a pint of water underneath them at 400°F/200°C/180°C/Gas Mark 6/middle of the Aga roasting oven for 45–50 minutes, removing the paper for the last 10 minutes. Check they are cooked through by piercing the thigh and checking the juices are clear. If you're using large poussin, split them in half and serve them skin side up over their portion of the stuffing. The juices in the pan make a delicious light gravy. You can thicken them if you like with a little cornflour and cream.

< 140 >

MIXED MEATBALLS WITH PASTA

In Umbria these *polpettini* are made from a variety of meats with veal usually included. As minced veal is not very common in the UK, I've suggested minced turkey. If you can get veal, do use it, as I think the flavour is better. This is a robust mountain dish that also goes well with polenta slices grilled.

Serves 4.

Ingredients

1 large slice wholemeal bread, broken into chunks
225 g/8 oz each minced turkey and beef
1 garlic clove, chopped
Juice and rind of 1 lemon
1 egg yolk
½ tsp each chopped fresh oregano and basil
1 tbsp tomato purée
675 g/1½ lb leeks, trimmed and thinly sliced
4 tbsp olive oil
400 g/14 oz can chopped tomatoes
Salt and freshly ground black pepper
Tagliatelle to serve

Method

Whizz the bread in a food processor or liquidizer. Remove half the breadcrumbs and add the turkey, garlic, lemon rind and egg yolk and process for 5–10 seconds until mixed. Clean out the bowl and chill the turkey mixture for 20 minutes. Add the beef to the food processor with the rest of the bread, the oregano, tomato purée and seasoning and process briefly until well combined. Chill for 20 minutes. Meanwhile, fry the leeks in half the olive oil until softened. Add the tomatoes, lemon juice and basil, mix well and cook gently for 10 minutes. Divide each meat mixture into eight portions and roll into balls – wet your hands to stop it sticking. Take a large, deep frying pan into which they will all fit, heat the remaining olive oil and fry the meatballs until lightly browned and firm. Add the leek and tomato mixture, reduce to a very low heat and simmer for 25–30 minutes. Serve at once in wide-rimmed bowls with the tagliatelle.

< 141 >

GRILLED FRUIT WITH MASCARPONE

This sweet, upside-down gratin can be made with any of the summer fruits either alone or in combination. I particularly like the combination of red fruits I've suggested here. But apricots or peaches or sliced fresh figs go equally well with the rich mascarpone base.

Ingredients

175 g/8 oz each strawberries, raspberries and redcurrants
50 g/2 oz caster sugar   **1 tbsp vanilla essence**
225 g/8 oz mascarpone cheese

Method

Mix 30 g/1 oz of the sugar into the mascarpone with the vanilla essence and level it into a gratin dish or china tart mould about 15–18 cm/6–7 in across. Hull and rinse the fruit – if the strawberries are big, slice them into quarters. Mix the fruit together and spread on the cheese. Sprinkle the remaining sugar over and put under a hot grill for 4–5 minutes until the sugar is caramelizing and the fruit is bubbling. Serve hot with crisp, thin biscuits.

< 142 >

RICOTTA WITH COFFEE

This is inspired by a recipe that Claudia Rodin discovered in Umbria and reports in her wonderful book, *The Food of Italy*. I suspect it's quite a recent development where ricotta, the Italian low fat whey cheese, is mixed with sugar and ground coffee as an end to a meal. She suggests that it can also be served as a do-it-yourself pudding, with ricotta being offered, and sugar and coffee, and a bottle of rum for individual mixing in individual bowls. It seems a little severe to me, even for the hardy mountain folk of Umbria and the Marches, but the flavour combination of coffee and ricotta is quite delicious, and I suggest here a slightly milder way of combining them. If you fancy the crunch of ground coffee in the dessert, do add a teaspoon or two of very finely ground expresso beans. A light sprinkling of ground coffee is, I must admit, about my limit, though it is very decorative.

Ingredients

225 g/8 oz ricotta
1 coffee cup full of strongly made expresso coffee
4 tbsp double cream
50 g/2 oz caster sugar
1 tsp ground expresso coffee, uncooked

Method

Mix the sugar into the hot strong coffee. Whip the cream until it's very thick and add the coffee and sugar mixture, spoonful by spoonful, attempting to keep as much air in the mixture as possible. Stir this into the ricotta, mixing it reasonably thoroughly but allowing a little marbling to remain. Spoon it into individual wine glasses and top with a sprinkling of ground coffee. Chill thoroughly before serving.

< 143 >

L'Aquila

< 144 >

ABRUZZI

Abruzzi is an ancient and little known part of Italy. Ancient because there are traces in this region of man's ancestors going back a million years, probably the oldest humanoid traces in the whole of Europe. And ancient too because there is evidence of modern human habitation going back 13,000 years and flourishing indigenous civilisations contemporary with ancient Greece. Since then however things have got quieter, although in Roman times, and subsequently under the Holy Roman Empire in the Middle Ages, the area was occasionally enlivened by contest. The great chain of the Apennines that runs through it down to the sea has both isolated and prevented it from attracting large populations or conquerors to prey on them. It is a very dramatic landscape with small villages not nestling in hills but huddled under great peaks on which the snow never melts, even in high summer. Even to Italians it's mostly known as a winter sports centre and a place for climbers though the beaches along the Adriatic coast are a major attraction, but the villages and towns that dot the countryside between still conduct themselves very much in the traditional old manner. In fact Abruzzi, since the 1960s, is divided into two regions: Abruzzi and Molise to the south. The recent arrival of the autostrada in the Abruzzi region is fuelling development, but Molise still remains very much one of the least known or visited places in Italy. The climate of the region varies considerably too. Because of the height of the mountains many of the towns are snowbound for months, and the whole region, except on the coast, is cooler than one would expect for somewhere so far south.

With so many mountains it is not really surprising that lamb is the great meat of the area, although mutton is still widely consumed as well. There's a lot of game, with hare and pheasant being amongst the favourites. They make a little pasta here, particularly the famous Maccheroni alla Chitarra, a kind of coarse cut, home-made pasta that requires a special wire strung device that looks (though doesn't sound) like a guitar to cut it. What little wheat is grown in the area is made into pasta using mountain water, which to many gourmets' minds makes it very sought after. The overwhelming characteristic of the cooking however comes from much further afield and is a passion for little hot chilli peppers. They appear in all kinds of recipes with almost all kinds of food except sweet ones. They are cooked fresh, dried and in a powdered form, and give the cooking of the whole region an unexpected and quite vivid pungency. Just why they should be so popular in this part of Italy is difficult to identify, as there are no traditions or connections

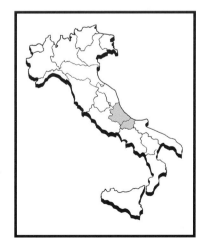

< 145 >

between the area and Mexico, or even with the Portuguese who were assiduous in carrying chillies around the globe from their New World colonies.

The coastal villages each have their own version of the fish soup or stew that was always the support of fishermen after they'd sold the best of their catch elsewhere. Just like in France these fishermen's stews have now taken on an almost ritually symbolic air of true cooking. The ones in Abruzzi and in Molise have an unusual characteristic for this part of Italy, in that they almost never contain tomatoes and are always cooked *a bianco*. This habit extends to fish sauces made to go with pasta and to fish risottos. There are however some unusual fish dishes including one known as Scapece which has some very ancient roots and is flavoured with saffron. Despite the lack of tomato these fish sauces and soups do not escape without the chilli pepper. Nor too do some extraordinary salamis, often made from liver and offal and mixed with what must be a Roman inheritance of honey, nuts and peel. There's quite a lot of cheese made in the area, and it is often cooked in what for Italy is a very unusual way, which is as thick slices grilled as a first course. Scamorza or Caciocavallo are worth looking out for; they're heated until they're bubbling and placed on country bread and sprinkled generously with black pepper before being consumed at the beginning of a meal.

A lot of very good vegetables are grown in the area, some of them quite unusual. Charred and bitter tubers that look and taste like a slightly charred onion are popular, as are endive, celery and fennel. In fact l'Aquila, the capital of Abruzzi, is famous for its celery (and for its trout which are fished in the mountain streams). The area also produces some very good olive oil.

Despite its strongly flavoured and idiosyncratic nature however it's not the food and the cooking of the region that are famous so much as the cooks themselves, especially those from the village of Villa Santa Maria, situated high in the mountains on the banks of the river Sangro. The village owes its tradition as a cooking centre and a centre for cooks to the Neapolitan princes who used to retreat up to the cool mountains here during the summers of the sixteenth century. They liked the local cooking so much they took some of the boys back with them to cook in their kitchens in the great houses in Naples. Kings and emperors (and Italian dictators) have all had cooks from Villa Santa Maria. In this century a cookery school proper was started in the village, and in recent years it has become a catering institute and a state hotel where young men and women are trained from the neighbourhood, from all over Italy and, indeed, from around the globe. I think though it's still worth exploring, when you're in the region, the cooking that first led those perspicacious princes to regard the food of the area as worth transferring to the palaces in Naples and Mantua.

< 146 >

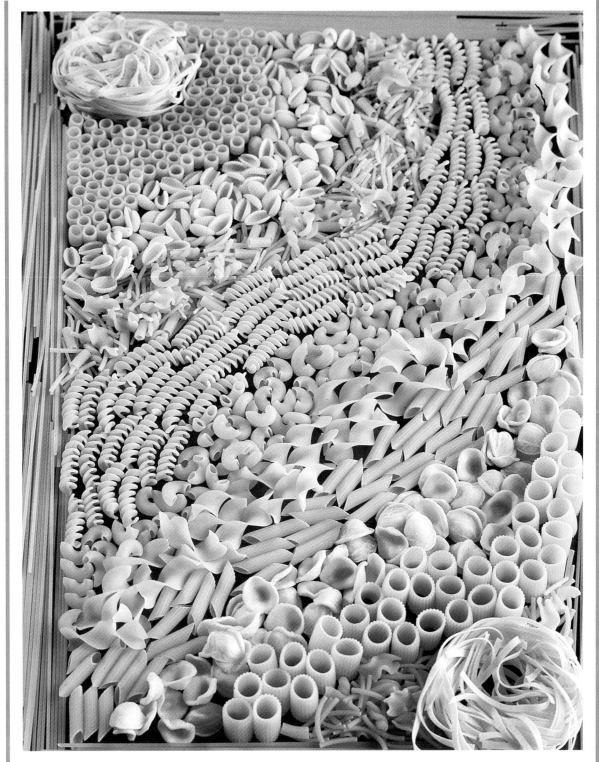

A pasta picture

< **147** >

EATING OUT

Along the coastline, as so often in Italy, the best bet is to look for the fishermen's trattoria, where little specialities and fish soups and stews will be easily found. Cooking in this area will tend to be rustic with an emphasis on the grill, especially for things like sardines, and on the pickled fish specialities. The *a bianco* fish risottos are also worth trying. Inland, the bigger towns have their own share of restaurants and local dishes are often to be found. Particularly in the winter look for casseroles and rich dishes made with the lentils that are a speciality of the region and famous all over Italy for their quality. Look too for pasta cooked simply, as the quality of the basic ingredient itself is held to be at its highest in this part of Italy, especially the Maccheroni alla Chitarra which can be found in some of the restaurants up in the mountainous region. Look also for the unusual soups made of the bitter green vegetables like escarole and cardoons. The town of Soumona, the birthplace of the Latin erotic poet Ovid, today specializes in confetti – sugared almonds that have been made here for hundreds of years. They are also a good buy to bring home with you. And in Teramo look for the very ancient tradition of *scrippelle*, thin pancakes which are used instead of pasta both in soup and to make a kind of local lasagne. The local cheeses are very varied but do not travel well. The one that is most used for cooking is *Scamorza*, which is smoked or grilled, usually as a first course. It is robust enough to bring home.

< 148 >

LA VIRTU

The name of this amazing soup from Teramo translates as 'virtue, rectitude or strength', and when you see the list of ingredients and taste the richness of the final product, you realize why it might have acquired such a reputation. As with many country soups, the detailed recipe varies from cook to cook and kitchen to kitchen, but the main ingredients of pasta, chick peas and a range of vegetables are central to it. It seems, to me at least, to be not so much a soup to start a meal with, as one to make a meal of. I think that very little else is needed, except perhaps some of the grilled cheese of the region (mozzarella makes a very good substitute) eaten on a slice of bread as a follow up, perhaps with a little fruit, to make a very substantial meal indeed. Meat is sometimes added to the soup, usually in the form of pork, but I prefer it just made with chicken stock. It is substantial enough already.

Ingredients

225 g/8 oz dried chick peas
225 g/8 oz soup pasta (little broken bits or the tiny shells known as *cabatieddi*)

1 chicken carcass or 1 lb chicken wings	Salt
1 large onion	4 sticks of celery
2 carrots	1 clove of garlic
1 sprig of rosemary	3 bay leaves
100 ml/4 fl oz olive oil	1 tsp chilli powder (to taste)

Method

Soak the chick peas overnight in plenty of water. Bring to the boil and simmer for 1 hour (you can use tinned chick peas which are strained and rinsed and start at this point in the recipe, and you will need 1 lb of tinned chick peas). Drain the chick peas and keep them. Put the chicken carcass and half the onion with its washed peel still on, 2 sticks of celery, 1 carrot, half the clove of garlic, a couple of bay leaves and the whole sprig of rosemary into a pan. Cover with 1.75 litres/3 pints of water, bring to the boil, skim the surface and leave to simmer for another 45 minutes. Remove the chicken. You can take the meat off the carcass or bones, and add it to the soup at the end, if you wish. Remove and discard the vegetables and the bay leaves and rosemary. Finely chop the remaining vegetables and sauté them in the olive oil for 2–3 minutes with the chilli powder. Start with half a teaspoon and go from there. Salt generously and pour over the soup and chick peas. Add the pasta, bring to the boil and simmer for 10 minutes until the pasta is thoroughly cooked, and the whole soup amalgamated. You may need to add a little more water. Sprinkle with a little parsley.

< 149 >

TOMATO, PRAWN AND ROCKET SALAD

Try to use the smallest cherry tomatoes you can find for this salad. They are often sold under names like Gardener's Delight or Flavia both of which have a bright, full colour. Rocket is now readily available and has an oak leaf sort of shape and a slightly spicy flavour and texture. Used in small quantities as it is in this salad, it adds colour and bite to the mixture. It's often gathered wild in Abruzzi.

Serves 4 as a starter.

Ingredients

225 g/8 oz small cherry tomatoes
3 tbsp sunflower oil
Pinch of salt
1 tsp Dijon mustard

100 g/4 oz rocket leaves
1 tbsp red wine vinegar
Pinch of sugar
175 g/6 oz cooked peeled prawns

Method

Discard any stalks on the tomatoes and cut each one in half. Wash and dry the rocket leaves and tear them into pieces. Put the oil, vinegar, salt, sugar and mustard in a screw-topped jar or small bowl and shake or whisk until smoothly blended. Lightly toss the tomatoes, rocket and prawns together and pile into individual serving dishes. Drizzle over the dressing and chill for about 30 minutes for the flavours to combine. Serve straight from the fridge.

< 150 >

(anticlockwise from the back) Pasta with raw tomato sauce p. 227; insalata di pesci p. 154; gorgonzola alla creme p. 17; tagliatelli & artichoke gratin p. 175; orecchiette with rape p. 210; spaghetti with oil, garlic and chilli p. 152

< 151 >

SPAGHETTI WITH OIL, GARLIC AND CHILLI

This dish has a number of different names in different parts of the area. It is sometimes known as Zappatora. In other places it's known by a more descriptive name of Aglio Olio e Pepperocimo. Either way it's very simple, very, very Italian and very pungent.

Serves 4.

Ingredients

350 g/12 oz spaghetti
6 tbsp olive oil

4 fat cloves of garlic
2 fresh ripe red chilli peppers

Salt and pepper

Method

Cook the spaghetti in boiling salted water for 3–4 minutes. Take off the heat and allow to stand with the lid on while you prepare the sauce. The pasta will be ready in about 6–7 minutes from the time you stop it cooking on the stove. Peel and crush the garlic with salt until you have a coarse purée. Heat the oil in a pan gently and add the garlic purée to it. Let it warm, but do not let it fry until it's brown. Depending on how hot you like your spaghetti, split the chillies and, if you like moderation, get rid of the seeds. The seeds are quite the hottest part! Rough chop the chilli and add that to the oil and garlic mixture, turning it until the aromas of both the chilli and the garlic rise from the oil, but it is not frying hard. When the spaghetti is *al dente*, drain it thoroughly and rinse it through with a pint of cold water. Put the spaghetti into a bowl, it will still be warm, and tip over the garlic, oil and chilli mixture. Turn thoroughly and serve immediately. Whether or not to use grated cheese with this is very much a matter of taste, but I must admit a preference for a little cheese to even out the pungency of the flavours. Black pepper is always turned fresh out of the mill liberally over the pasta when it's been served in portions.

< 152 >

LINGUINE WITH WALNUTS

This dish uses an unusual combination of flavours to dress the fine, square-shaped spaghetti of the region. In fact, walnuts and basil are a combination also known on the other side of Italy in Genoa where there are recipes for pesto (the famous green sauce) that uses walnuts instead of the more traditional pine nuts. It makes a surprisingly satisfying dish with a strong rich flavour.

Serves 4.

Ingredients

350 g/12 oz linguine pasta

100 g/4 oz walnut halves

Juice of half a lemon

50ml/2 fl oz olive oil

Handful fresh basil leaves

Salt and freshly ground black papper

Freshly grated parmesan, to serve

Method

Place the pasta in a large pan of boiling salted water and cook for 3 minutes, then remove from the heat and leave to stand for 7 minutes. Drain well, reserving 200 ml/7 fl oz of the cooking water and mix the pasta with the olive oil. Place in a serving bowl and keep warm. Place the reserved cooking water in a food processor or liquidizer with most of the walnuts and whizz to a fine but not completely smooth texture. Cut the basil into thin ribbons and toss into the pasta with the walnut sauce. Season to taste and sprinkle over the lemon juice. Scatter over the remaining walnuts and a little parmesan and serve at once.

INSALATA DI PESCI

Salads made with fish seem to be an Italian phenomenon. There are cold fish dishes in other places, but the wonderful great oval plates of dressed fish, prawns and pasta together seem to be something I have never found outside Italy. It's a dish for the summer months when fish is plentiful and cold food like this welcome. It is, however, worth saying that this is a very rich

< 153 >

and quite filling dish, wonderful for parties, because it has both the ability to be laid out in a buffet and also to be eaten with just a fork while you hold the plate with another hand. The fish of the Adriatic coasts are not readily available here, but I have suggested substitutes that are either appropriate or equivalent in terms of texture.

Ingredients

450 g/1 lb firm fleshed white fish (monkfish or haddock or huss)   **2 red mullet**
225 g/8 oz tiger prawns (cooked or raw with shell on but no heads)   **1 lemon**
275 g/10 oz small pasta (farfalle, the little bows or the little   **1 bay leaf**
    elbow-shaped macaroni are ideal)   **½ onion**
225 g/8 oz lemon flavoured mayonnaise   **1 tbsp olive oil**
1 tbsp fennel feathers, finely chopped

Method

Make a little poaching liquid for the fish with the juice of half the lemon, the bay leaf and the half onion and about a pint of cold water and a pinch of salt. Into this place the white fish, the red mullet, and the prawns if they are raw. Bring to the boil and simmer for about 5 minutes. Switch off and allow the fish to cool in the water. If you need to shell the prawns, do this. Flake the white fish and remove the fillets from the red mullet, discarding the skin and all the debris. You can, if you wish, put all of this back into the stock and boil it again for another 10 or 15 minutes to intensify the flavour, as it is going to be part of the sauce. Cook the pasta in plenty of boiling salted water until it's just tender. This will depend on the thickness of the pasta but shouldn't take more than 8–9 minutes. Drain thoroughly and rinse under cold water so that it doesn't stick. Stir a tablespoon of olive oil into the pasta and place it in a bowl. Add to the pasta the flaked white fish and the finely chopped fennel and two thirds of the mayonnaise and mix thoroughly together. Use this to fill the centre of an oval platter, to a depth of about an inch. Break up the red mullet fillets roughly and mix those with the cooked prawns. Place those in the half moons on either side of the central column of fish and pasta. Squeeze the juice from the remaining half of lemon over the prawns and mullet. Dilute the remaining mayonnaise with 2 or 3 tablespoons of the strained fish stock and pour that over the mullet and prawn sides of the dish. You may decorate the dish, if you wish, with baby tomatoes, thin slices of lemon and sprigs of fennel before serving it. Make sure everyone gets a bit of both kinds of the salad.

< 154 >

ROAST LAMB WITH MINT

This way of cooking lamb comes by way of Claudia Rodin from the great cookery school in Villa Santa Maria. I've adapted it slightly but it's interesting to see the ancient British combination of mint and lamb reappearing in this unusual and quite spectacular version.

Ingredients

1 x 2.5 kg/5 lb leg of lamb, boned (get your butcher to do it if you can)

2 cloves of garlic	1 large bunch of mint
2 sticks of celery	1 large onion
2 carrots	1 lemon
Salt and pepper	4 tbsp olive oil

Method

If your lamb isn't boned, do it along the bony side of the lamb, opening it out lengthways. A sharp knife and a little patience should produce a piece of meat with a gap in the middle that you can spread with the garlic, peeled and crushed, and half the mint, well chopped. Roll the leg together again and tie it 2 or 3 times with a piece of string. Heat a roasting tin with the olive oil in. Peel the onion and the carrots and cut them into quarters. Add those to the tin when the oil is hot and the celery, cut into 2.5 cm/1 in lengths. Place the leg of lamb on top of the vegetables, sprinkle with salt and pepper and the juice of the lemon. Cook at 375°F/190°C/180°C Fan/Gas Mark 5/bottom of the roasting oven in the Aga, for 1 hour 45 minutes. This will produce meat that's pink at the centre. Another quarter of an hour should just cook the lamb through, but more will be too much and will make the meat tough. Remove from the pan and allow to stand covered with a piece of foil while you make the sauce. Add a little water or stock to the pan to take up the sediment and mix that and the vegetables together in a food processor. Purée to make a sauce about the thickness of single cream. Add the remaining mint leaves to the food processor and blend those in. Slice the lamb in thick pieces and serve with the sauce and potatoes or pasta as your preference takes you.

< 155 >

AGNELLO ALL' ARRABBIATA

Just why this dish is named after the Arabs is anybody's guess because it's for certain that it wasn't they who brought the fiery chillies that are its most typical ingredient to Italy. However, all dishes in this part of Italy that have the particular combination of chilli, rosemary and garlic have the *Arrabbiata* suffix, so perhaps it's simply an association with exotic flavours. This is a real rustic dish and the lamb used in it is often rather more what we would call mutton with a substantial and strong flavour of its own. I find the rather darker lamb that comes from New Zealand makes an excellent substitute in Britain. It's also not at any level a refined dish, the lamb being cut in chunks and served in generous portions. Accompaniments are often sautéd potatoes as some of the sauce from the lamb can be served with an earlier dish of pasta, though the pasta would make a good alternative to the potatoes if you prefer.

Ingredients

900 g/2 lb lamb, cut into 5 cm/2 in pieces off the bone (leg or shoulder depending on your inclination)
450 g/1 lb ripe tomatoes or 1 tin of chopped Italian tomatoes in juice

4 cloves of garlic	2 fresh red chilli peppers (or 3 dried ones)
4 tbsp olive oil	1 large onion
2 sprigs of rosemary	Salt and pepper

Method

Peel and finely chop the onion and garlic. Split the peppers and, unless you really like hot food, remove the seeds. Rough chop the flesh. If you're using fresh tomatoes, split them, squeeze out any surplus seeds and juice and cut them into quarters. Heat the oil in a dish that will go in the oven and add the lamb chunks and cook over a medium heat until they're golden all over. Sprinkle over the garlic, onions and chillies and stir, allowing the vegetables to turn translucent but not to burn. Add the tomatoes and, if needed, a tablespoon or two of water. Season generously, add the rosemary, cover and place in a slow oven, 325°F/170°C/160°C Fan/Gas Mark 3/top of the simmering oven in the Aga, for 1½ hours until the meat is absolutely tender and the sauce has amalgamated to a rich, dark juice. You may want to stir the dish once during the cooking to make sure that the whole amalgamation takes place thoroughly. Check for seasoning and serve in deep dishes so that plenty of sauce can come with the chunks of lamb.

< 156 >

Agnello all'arrabbiata p. 156

< 157 >

GRILLED SARDINES

Fresh sardines are now very widely available, I've seen them everywhere from supermarkets to fish shops. They are eaten all over Italy of course but the ones from the Adriatic are often held to have the best flavour.

Serves 4.

Ingredients

8 x 100–175 g/4–6 oz fresh sardines
2 tbsp olive oil
1 lemon, quartered
8 rosemary sprigs
Salt and freshly ground black pepper
Mixed green salad, to serve

Method

Preheat the grill (or barbecue) to maximum for at least 10 minutes. Brush the sardines with the oil and squeeze the lemon juice over them. Leave to stand for at least 10 minutes while the grill heats. Place a piece of foil on the grill – this will make a big difference to the washing up – and place the sardines on that foil, pouring a little of the marinade over them. Grill close to the flame for 3–4 minutes or until the skins bubble and blister. Turn the sardines and put a piece of rosemary on each one, pour over a little more of the marinade and grill for another 3–4 minutes until cooked through. When they're done, place them on warmed plates and season generously. Serve at once with the salad.

< 158 >

Grilled sardines p. 158

< 159 >

RABBIT IN A CASSEROLE

This style of game cooking is used for both fur and feathers, with some small adjustments depending on the exact nature of the animal and the time of year. It's also used, with the addition of tomatoes, for cooking chicken and other feathered game in a style known as *cacciatori* or hunter style. The method of cooking is also known as *in tegame* in the region. Rabbit is eaten much more widely in Italy than it is in Britain and if you or your family are squeamish about this, you could easily substitute pheasant or even pigeon.

Ingredients

900 g/2 lb rabbit
3 tbsp olive oil
1 small onion
1 clove of garlic
2 sprigs of rosemary
1 big sprig of sage
1 lemon
300 ml/½ pint of stock or water
Salt and pepper

Method

Cut the rabbit into 8 pieces (or do the same with a pheasant and split the pigeons in half). Brown them lightly in the olive oil, season generously with salt and pepper, add the rosemary and sage and the chopped onion and garlic. Squeeze over the lemon juice and add the grated rind of the lemon. Moisten with the stock or water (they might also use white or even red wine in Abruzzi) and simmer gently covered, on top of the stove, for 20–25 minutes until cooked through. The sauce should be much reduced. If the meat is done before that is the case, remove it from the heat and reduce the sauce by fierce boiling. Serve with something to soak up the juices – rice, mashed potato or even, though it's not local, polenta.

< 160 >

CHOCOLATE AMARETTI MOUSSE

This is a quite wonderful mousse, made with amaretti biscuits that are flavoured with apricot kernels and little almonds. As you eat this mousse you get this wonderful creamy, chocolatey texture and then hit the crunchy, slightly bitter flavour of the biscuits. It is quite appallingly wonderful! It is, however, made with raw eggs, so I fear it is not for the elderly, the pregnant, or the very young, at least if you are making it in Britain and following government advice.

Serves 4.

Ingredients

175 g/6 oz bitter chocolate, with at least 50% cocoa solids

Juice and grated rind of 1 orange

50 g/2 oz unsalted butter

6 eggs

6 amaretti biscuits, crushed

Method

Break the chocolate into small pieces and place it in a non-stick pan with the orange juice and rind. Then gently melt the chocolate into the orange juice, stirring occasionally until smooth and glossy. Remove from the heat. Separate the eggs. Add the butter to the chocolate mixture, and allow it to melt in the existing heat, then stir until well blended. Add the egg yolks and stir until well combined. Whip the egg whites in a separate bowl until they are so thick you can turn the bowl upside down. Then carefully, knocking as little air out of the egg whites as you can, fold the egg whites into the chocolate mixture. Spoon half the mousse into wine glasses. Sprinkle over half of the amaretti biscuits and spoon on the remaining mousse. Sprinkle the remaining biscuits on top. Place in the fridge for at least two hours to set.

< 161 >

Vatican guard

< 162 >

ROME

Rome, according to the cliché 'the eternal city', is certainly the only city in the whole world to have remained a capital for nearly 2,500 years. When the vigorous, brutal and highly organized city of Rome first emerged about 400 BC to challenge the domination of the region by the Etruscans, it was just one amongst many city states. By the time of the birth of Christ its Empire stretched from the North Atlantic to the Sahara Desert and from the Portuguese Coast to Egypt. It was during that century that Augustus, the first of the Emperors taking over from the ancient republican traditions, turned Rome from what he described as a city built of brick to 'a city built of marble'. Today many of those monuments and buildings still remain, or at least impressive and emotive fragments of them do. Rome went on to rule its great Empire for another 400 years. Briefly after its fall to the Barbarians in the fifth century it ceased to be a capital, but then the Popes emerged and made it their capital, and gradually through the Middle Ages its authority, spiritual rather than physical most of the time, grew until once again it became in the nineteenth century the capital of the united Italy.

As well as always being a capital city Rome has had one other singular advantage and that is for all of that 2,500 years it's had paved roads. That may seem a superficial thought, but it is more than just a tribute to the extraordinary engineering of the Roman legions. It means that Rome has always had access to other peoples and, not least important, sources of food. Easy access was truly significant during the Middle Ages when villagers could starve five miles from plenty as winter storms and muddy roads prevented wagons moving. It also means that Rome has comparatively little cooking of its own; it has been influenced not only by hundreds of thousands of immigrants from its national provinces, but also from people all around the world. Rome's province, Lazio, along the western coast, has quite a long coastline but is so dominated by the great city itself that such traditions of local cooking which exist tend to be very simple.

Listing the wonders of the city is almost impossible. Many of the ancient Roman ruins have been restored or at least exposed: the great complex around the Forum, and the baths and arches and columns which one finds around almost every turning in the ancient part of the city. The Rostra, where Cicero spoke, still stands as does much of the extraordinary Coliseum, but so too does the Pantheon, a building the size of whose dome is awesome even now. Then there is the medieval Rome of the Popes, leading to the extraordinary flowering of the Renaissance, particularly in the great

< 163 >

buildings and paintings of the Vatican itself. The Sistene Chapel is famous in its own right, but there are still whole squares designed by Michelangelo and untouched since his time. There are many and beautiful fountains, of which the Trevi is only one, and the marvellous parks, particularly the Borgese Park built on the site of that family's estate.

Classical Roman cooking, from what we know of it, was highly spiced and, certainly at banquet level, very complicated, with peacocks being cooked and then redressed in their feathers, six or seven different animals or birds being stuffed inside each other, and such extraordinary delicacies as lark's tongue really being eaten as serious courses. Apicus, the gourmet writer whose works are the only ones to survive in significant quantity from that time, clearly liked a good party and wrote about the kind of cooking and events which, even in Rome's great days, only about two hundred or so of the richest families and the Imperial Court could enjoy. More day-to-day cooking revolved around a wide consumption of vegetables and lots of bread and, unusually for that period, bread based almost exclusively on wheat. Flavourings were interesting in that garum, a liquid sauce highly salted and made from fermented anchovies, was a central seasoning. The use of anchovies and their saltiness is today a strong memory of that particular sort of process, as many of the dishes that Romans regard as their own have anchovies added to them. Vegetables are still a Roman passion, particularly their beloved artichokes and peas. The artichokes tend to come in a variety of colours and sizes, but are generally small. So small in some cases that they can be eaten raw, just sliced into salads or cooked whole and eaten in the same way. Don't be tempted to try either of those tricks with the artichokes available in this country because they are too tough and the central choke must be removed before ours can be consumed. But in Rome, cooked with mint and peas, or in the Jewish style, trimmed and deep fried whole, they are often part of the widely available *antipasti*.

Pasta too comes from other places as there's little original pasta from Rome. It tends to be pasta longha, in the form of spaghetti or tagliatelle and usually eaten with tomato-based sauces except for the famous carbonara sauce where eggs, cream and pancetta, bacon or salami are mixed together, allowing the heat of the pasta to cook the eggs and cream sauce in the bowl. There is some fish eaten but despite the long coastline there's not really much seafood cookery in the city. When they're not eating vegetables it's meat that Romans really like, particularly young or baby lamb eaten when it's still milk fed. This produces very small joints and tiny chops but that doesn't stop them being cooked and eaten with relish across the city, as is baby goat or kid – *caprito* – in season. Indeed near the old abattoirs (recently moved) in the centre of the city there are a number of restaurants specializing in unusual parts of the animal. The recipes served there include a wide range of what's known as the fifth quarter of the animal.

Civita Bagnoreggio

< 164 >

The fifth quarter was the offal – the trotters, liver, intestines and tail of the many animals killed to feed the appetites of the great and good for whom Rome has always been a magnet. Princes and cardinals and senators ate the best cuts leaving the offal for the poor to enjoy. As is so often the case, the poor's method of dealing with this largesse has turned into some of the most fashionable eating in the city, and parts of animals that you may not have been conscious of existing as culinary options can be found cooked in both family and restaurant kitchens. Oxtail cooked with grapes, and trotters are amongst the most famous of these dishes. Some other meat, especially veal, is eaten, particularly in the famous Saltimboca, or 'jump in the mouth', a little confection of veal escalope rolled round ham and sometimes cheese and cooked in little parcels. Big grilled veal chops also seem to be a speciality of the area.

The city itself has regions in it for its cooking traditions. One of the most interesting being that of the Jewish quarter right on the Tiber in the centre of the ancient city where, despite the deportation of many Jews during the fascist regime, there is still a tradition of cooking in the kosher style. This includes the famous baccala or fried salted cod sticks, zucchini flowers stuffed and deep fried and, most famous of all, the Jewish style artichokes, flattened until they resemble water lilies and then deep fried. They also specialize in pasta dishes cooked with vegetables, their version of the obsession with vegetables that permeates Roman cookery.

Across the river from the ancient city stands the centre that kept Rome a capital for over a thousand years, the Vatican, a city in its own right inside Rome. Here also is the Trastevere, a medieval city of alleyways and roads leading towards the sudden extraordinary open space of St Peter's Square. There is a cooking style of its own in this part of town too, particularly the little restaurants and trattoria specializing in the simple *cucina di povere* that the Roman people feel that they have always practised in the shadow of their masters. The immigration of hundreds of thousands from the other provinces means that a lot of domestic and restaurant cooking in Rome reflects the other regions very strongly.

Everywhere there's a particular liking for baby vegetables, and indeed baby salads, with some specially grown mixtures being picked with the leaves the size of only a finger, before being dressed in oil and lemon juice with a little salt and pepper and nothing much else. The Roman use of herbs is somewhat unusual in that in a number of dishes they use mint as a cooking rather than as a decorative herb. Not with lamb usually, strangely enough, but with the self-same artichokes and also with fish, particularly with grilled fish, adding a sharp, almost citrus-like note to the richness of the flesh.

< 165 >

Civita Bagnoreggio

< 166 >

EATING OUT

The Romans take eating out both very seriously and very casually. Rather like the Japanese, very few Romans entertain at home as the city's enormous variety of restaurants is regarded as the normal place to entertain your guests. This of course doesn't apply to families but even there there is a tradition on high days and holidays of eating 'outside the walls' at a series of osteria or trattoria which specialize in these kinds of parties. The Roman climate encourages outdoor eating; therefore every restaurant, café and snack bar has tables outside whenever it can, often in the middle of quite busy, traffic-filled and noisy streets. There are wonderful oases as well, often to be found in the back streets on the 'other' side of the town, the Trastevere, where only the motor scooter can penetrate. But look too at some of the more expensive restaurants, many of which have charming gardens, often in places where you can look at two thousand years of history laid out in architectural glory in front of you.

If you stay away from the more obvious tourist haunts around the bottom of the Spanish Steps or some of the restaurants in the grander hotels, you can eat very well, comparatively cheaply. Garlic, often regarded as the fuel of the legions, is still present in most savoury dishes; from the simplest of bruschetta and spaghetti, through to grander, more complicated confections pounded with anchovies and other ingredients. In sauces both for meat and vegetable dishes, garlic abounds. Speaking of vegetable dishes, these are one of the great prides of Rome, and you will find all kinds in a wide variety of *antipasti*, often laid out on a table for you to help yourself. They will almost certainly include artichokes in a variety of forms, usually much smaller and more delicate than the artichokes we can get in Britain. They're often eaten whole, sometimes even in their very small state raw, just in a salad dressing, but often cooked with peas and mint, and sometimes in the tradition from the Jewish quarter, *carciofi alla giudia*, opened, de-choked and deep fried. While there is pasta on the menu it is usually egg pasta, served with a comparatively light sauce, often surprisingly flavoured with the chillies from the nearby Abruzzi.

The main meat dish is likely to be lamb, often milk-fed, another ancient Roman tradition. It's cooked in a variety of ways, perhaps most famously with rosemary and garlic, with a little tomato sauce and some potatoes. Tripe and oxtail make some of the cold weather stews and various bits of the lamb, including its intestines, are sometimes turned into grills to serve on pasta or rice. The Romans like deep-frying things: some of the best classic fritto mistos in Italy can be found here, with unexpected ingredients – brains, sweetbreads, liver, artichokes, apples, pears and even slices of stale bread dipped in milk.

The enthusiasm for vegetables is such that sometimes you'll find the most extraordinary and delicious raw combinations of baby vegetables and baby salad greens served with a variety of olive oil and/or vinaigrette dips often with bitter leaves like the rocket. Sometimes the

< 167 >

rocket is very simply boiled, allowed to go cold and then dressed with a salad dressing. Particularly on high days and holidays the Romans like eating and walking about and street vendor food can be common. Roasted meat off carts, rice balls with hot mozzarella inside them, and slices of pizza rustica, provide a mobile snack. Most of the fish eaten is either grilled or baked and served with lemon and often a butter sauce.

And as for fish so it is true for puddings. There are very few traditional Roman ways to end a meal apart from the marvellous fruit, both of the region and elsewhere. What Rome does specialize in is strawberries, both the tiny woodland kind and the larger, richer ones, often eaten in a very simple way with just a flavouring of sugar and a little lemon. There are pastry shops and indeed pastries on dessert carts in restaurants, but there's not much taste or enthusiasm for them. One of the best places to try them, if you fancy something like that, is in one of the cafés, which are also really little bars, all over the city.

The Forum

< 168 >

ROMAN CRUDITÉS

Pinzimonio is a dish often served in Roman homes and restaurants. It consists of a bowl of fresh vegetables which are dipped in a mixture of olive oil, salt and pepper and occasionally red wine vinegar. Usually these are presented in separate bowls, though sometimes they are mixed to a kind of vinaigrette which is shared at the centre of the table. People dip a piece of celery or whatever into the bowl, nibble it and dip again. It may not be hygienic but it certainly does have a simple and rustic appeal.

Ingredients

1 head of celery, separated
1 head of fennel
6 carrots
1 bunch of radishes, preferably with their leaves on
1 medium cucumber
225 ml/8 fl oz virgin olive oil
1 tsp salt
1 tsp ground black pepper
2 tbsp red wine vinegar
Assorted leaves, to dress the serving dish

Method

Trim the vegetables, separate the celery discarding any coarse outer stalks. Separate the fennel, splitting the larger 'cups' in half. Wash the radishes, trimming off the root part but leaving a little bit of the green stalk attached. Split the cucumber lengthwise, scoop out the seeds, cut each canoe in half and then cut again lengthwise into six batons, giving 24 pieces altogether. Peel the carrots and cut those lengthwise into 4 or 5 strips depending on their width. Arrange the vegetables in a sort of giant cartwheel on an oval or a round plate in the middle of which is a bowl with the olive oil. If you wish to stir the vinegar, salt and pepper into the oil to make a single dressing do so, if not serve those in smaller bowls around the edge for people to add to their dipping.

< 169 >

MIXED BRUSCHETTA PLATTER

A typical Roman snack, a classic bruschetta is a simple affair of grilled bread, rubbed all over with garlic and brushed generously with extra-virgin olive oil. However you can, of course, be more creative and top the toasts with all sorts of grand combinations. The flavours used here are all frequent partners, providing a selection of toppings and a very appetising way to start a meal.

Serves 6–8 as a starter.

Ingredients

2 ciabatta loaves
4–6 tbsp extra-virgin olive oil
1 large garlic clove, halved
4 plum tomatoes, sliced
50 g/2 oz can anchovy fillets, drained
2 tbsp shredded basil leaves
3 tbsp pesto sauce
150 g/6 oz fontina cheese
50 g/2 oz stuffed green olives

Method

Preheat the grill and cut each ciabatta into about fifteen slices, discarding the ends. Toast the bread lightly on both sides and rub all over on one side with the garlic. Brush liberally with olive oil. Arrange two or three slices of tomato on half of the toasts. Halve the anchovies and place two pieces in a criss-cross pattern on each one and garnish with shredded basil leaves. Spread the pesto on the remaining bruschetta. Slice the fontina or cut into small cubes and arrange on top of the pesto. Garnish with the olives. Serve warm.

< 170 >

Bruschetta p. 170

< 171 >

STRACIATELLA

Straciatella is the typical Roman soup. It's made from broth at home, and in fancy restaurants is a very carefully clarified and strained consommé. If you fancy this level of clarity you might want to buy tinned consommé which has already been clarified. I like making it with a good tasty chicken broth made from the carcass of a chicken and a little leek, onion, or carrot and bay leaf simmered for about an hour on the stove and strained carefully. Clarification always seems to me to be a little bit too refined for this basically peasant soup.

Ingredients

1.2 litres/2 pints of chicken stock or consommé
4 eggs
4 tbsp parmesan, coarsely grated
1 pinch of nutmeg (optional)

Method

Bring the stock or consommé to the boil. Turn the heat right down and while the stock is simmering add the nutmeg if you are using it. Beat the eggs in a bowl with a fork until well blended. Beat in the cheese and a pinch of salt. With the soup on the boil, but only just, pour the egg mixture into the hot soup in a steady stream, stirring vigorously with a fork to break it up into small strands. The soup should look like it's got very fine golden vermicelli in it by the time you've finished. Take it off the heat and allow to stand for a minute before serving. It needs nothing else except good bread.

ARTICHOKES WITH LEMON AND MINT

This is an adaptation of a Roman artichoke dish for our rather larger and coarser vegetables. Try and buy artichokes without any browning on the ends of their leaves. Younger and smaller ones are usually worth the extra cost. Traditionally, Romans stew their artichokes with mint, often with peas and wine and olive oil. I'm going to suggest a rather simpler way of

< 172 >

cooking them but adding mint to the lemon butter you dip them in when you eat them. Our artichokes can't be eaten whole as many of the Roman varieties can.

Ingredients

4 medium sized young artichokes
100 g/4 oz butter
1 tbsp finely chopped mint

1 tbsp red wine vinegar
Juice of 2 lemons

Method

Trim the artichokes cutting the tops of the leaves across to provide a flat head and trimming the stalk off level with the base. Put them into a pan of water acidulated with the red wine vinegar and bring to the boil. Salt when it boils and boil for between 10–15 minutes depending on how big and tough the artichokes are. The base should be pierced easily with a skewer when they're cooked. When cooked, remove them and drain them upside down in a colander for 2–3 minutes to allow as much water to run out as possible. Meanwhile melt the butter but don't let it come to the boil – it's not meant to turn oily. Whisk in the juice of the 2 lemons and then the finely chopped mint. If it's unsalted butter, you may want to add half a teaspoon of salt to the mixture. Place the artichokes, leaf side up, on individual plates and provide a small bowl or saucer for each person to have a portion of the butter and mint sauce to dip the base of the leaves into, and, finally, the artichoke heart, having removed the hairy choke as they eat it. This can be served cold but you'll have to substitute olive oil for the butter in the dressing.

PENNE CON MELANZANE

This dish of 'quill' pasta with aubergines is not really very Roman in that its flavours come from the South, but Rome is a city which has attracted recipes and people from all over the Italian peninsula, and this one it has taken well to its heart. It's quite a substantial dish, as most aubergine dishes are, and is quite capable of standing alone as a vegetarian main course.

< 173 >

Ingredients

450 g/1 lb pasta quills (penne)
2 tins of Italian tomatoes, not chopped but whole in juice
Small handful of basil leaves
2 oz parmesan cheese, grated

450 g/1 lb aubergines
100 g/4 oz butter
2 tbsp olive oil
2 cloves of garlic

Salt

Method

Trim the aubergines and cut them, unpeeled, into 1 cm/½ in slices. If they're very large, you might want to cut the slices in half again. Melt the butter in a saucepan with a close-fitting lid. Add the aubergines and cook gently, turning them over a couple of times for about 20 minutes. You may need to add a little water if they start to dry out. At the end of this time they should be quite soft and pureéd. Drain the tomatoes from their juice (keep their juice for something else) and cut each tomato into four. Heat the oil in a separate pan, add the tomatoes and then add the finely chopped garlic. Season generously with salt and perhaps a pinch of sugar to bring out the flavour of the tomatoes. Cook the penne in a large pan of boiling salted water for 3–4 minutes. Take off the heat, put the lid on and leave them to cook for 7 minutes. Drain the penne thoroughly and place in a bowl. Add the aubergine mixture, then the tomato mixture and the parmesan cheese. Toss together, sprinkle over the basil and serve immediately. You might want to have another bowl of cheese on the table for individual diners to add. Black pepper goes nicely with this as well.

PASTA CARBONARA

This is one of my favourite pasta dishes and it is effortlessly easy to make. It is supposed to be the kind of pasta Italian charcoal burners and coal miners liked – the *carbonari* – as it has a lovely, creamy fresh taste, perfect after working in dust. You can either use flat noodles, tagliatelle, or spirals, eliche. I use dried rather than fresh pasta for this and the whole thing takes just 10 minutes to cook. Versions exist using bacon or pancetta or salami. I find salami the nicest.

Serves 4.

< 174 >

Ingredients

350 g/12 oz tagliatelli or spiral pasta   A little olive oil
50 g/2 oz salami   6 tbsp single cream
50 g/2 oz freshly grated parmesan   2 large eggs
Salt and freshly ground black pepper

Method

Bring to the boil a large pan of water and add a pinch of salt and a little oil. Drop in the pasta. Cook it for 3 minutes then take it off the heat, put the lid on and leave it to one side. Cut the salami into matchsticks and place them in a separate pan. Fry them for 1–2 minutes in their own fat until they are slightly crisp. Beat together the cream and the eggs in a bowl. Seven minutes after you put the lid on the pasta and put it aside, drain. It will be perfectly cooked al dente. Place the pasta in a large bowl and pour over the cream mixture, stirring to coat. The heat from the pasta will cook the eggs and form a wonderful, thick, creamy sauce. Add the salami and seasoning and mix again until well combined. Serve at once in wide-rimmed bowls with some of the parmesan sprinkled on top and plenty of black pepper.

TAGLIATELLE AND ARTICHOKE GRATIN

Here Rome's favourite vegetable is combined with its favourite pasta in a rich gratin. The use of pesto – from Genoa originally – is typical of the metropolitan touch of using ingredients from other provinces to enliven the capital's foods.

Serves 4.

Ingredients

290 g/10 oz jar artichoke hearts preserved in oil or brine
300 ml/½ pint double cream   225 g/8 oz tagliatelle pasta
30 g/1 oz freshly grated parmesan   2 tbsp pesto sauce
Salt and freshly ground black pepper   2 eggs

< 175 >

Preparing tagliatelli & artichoke gratin p. 175

< 176 >

Method

Preheat the oven to 400°F/200°C/180°C Fan/Gas Mark 6/middle of the Aga roasting oven. Cook the pasta in a large pan of boiling salted water for 3 minutes. Take off the heat and set aside with the lid on for 7–8 minutes until just tender and cooked through. Drain the pasta, return to the pan and toss with the pesto sauce. Leave to cool. Meanwhile, drain the artichoke hearts and roughly chop. Mix together with the eggs, cream, seasoning and half of the parmesan until well combined. Add the artichoke hearts and egg mixture to the pasta and stir well to combine. Season to taste. Spoon into a baking dish and sprinkle over the remaining parmesan. Bake for 25–30 minutes until just set and lightly golden. Serve hot.

GRILLED MONKFISH WITH MINT

Monkfish is a fish often eaten in Rome but can work out quite expensive so you can very successfully substitute halibut or haddock instead. Mint is a herb not usually associated with fish but adds a piquant edge to it here.

Serves 4.

Ingredients

450 g/1 lb monkfish tail (or 4 halibut or haddock steaks)
2 tbsp chopped fresh mint
Juice of 1 lemon

2 garlic cloves
4 tsp olive oil
¼ tsp salt

Method

If your fishmonger is filleting the monkfish for you, ask him to cut it into four equal portions. Then make a cut along the length of each piece, not right the way through but just enough so it opens slightly. Crush the garlic with the salt and mix with the olive oil, lemon juice and mint in a shallow bowl. Add the fish, turn to coat and chill for at least 15 minutes or up to 1 hour is fine. Preheat the grill to maximum and cook the fish so that the top of it is at least 5 cm/2 in away from the grill. Cook for about 6–8 minutes under a high heat. If the fish is very thick, you may need to turn it over

< 177 >

to make sure it is fully cooked, otherwise turn the grill down and continue to cook for another 2–3 minutes until the fish is opaque and cooked all the way through. This is nicest served with a fresh green salad.

POLLO E PEPERONI IN PADEELA

Chicken isn't ever listed as a speciality of any of the Italian regions yet it's eaten throughout Italy and in all kinds of ways. What they're best at, though little renowned for, I think, is not the little fried chicken morsels that adorn so many restaurant menus, but the rich country stews that are made with the local vegetables. This one uses peppers rather than tomatoes to give the chicken colour and flavour. It's a cold weather as well as a warm weather dish, even Rome has some winter, and goes very well with fried potatoes, pasta or, occasionally, though it's not common in the city, rice.

Ingredients

1 chicken or 8 chicken pieces
1 clove of garlic
4 tbsp olive oil

1 medium sized Spanish onion
2 red and 2 yellow peppers
Small handful of fresh basil

Method

You can cook this recipe with either the whole chicken or joints. Traditionally it was done with the whole chicken but joints are perhaps easier. Peel and slice the onion finely and fry it in the oil in a large pan until it's soft but not brown. Finely chop the garlic and add that and then the chicken pieces. Cook them gently for about 5 minutes a side until they're thoroughly golden. Meanwhile, split the peppers, remove the seeds and stalk and slice them across into 1 cm/½ in pieces. Season the chicken generously when it's browned, add the peppers, stirring them into the mixture to pick up the flavours, and cook with the lid on over a low heat. You might want to use a heat diffuser if your stove doesn't turn down far enough. Cook for 25–30 minutes until the chicken is cooked through and the peppers are wilted but still whole. You may need to add a drop or two of water as this happens. Finely chop the basil and dish the chicken onto a pretty plate, sprinkle with the basil and serve immediately.

< 178 >

ABBACCHIO ALLA ROMANA

In Rome this is made with baby lamb, spring or milk fed lamb, a whole leg of which will barely feed three people. It's very difficult to find this special lamb in Britain but a leg of British lamb early in the year, before it develops too much size, is probably the best substitute. I first had this recipe in an Italian restaurant where it was supposed to be a speciality. Unfortunately, they appeared to run out of it halfway through the meal. It was only when I realized that almost all of the rest of the restaurant was occupied by one of the famous Italian football teams, all of whom were eating exactly the same dish, that I realized why I was lucky to get the last portion available from the kitchen. It's a stunning way of cooking lamb and although it uses the same basic ingredients as is used in French roast lamb, the result, somehow or other, comes out very differently.

Ingredients

1 x 1.2–1.4 kg/2½–3 lb leg of lamb, trimmed and with the saddle bone (at the thick end) cut out

4 cloves of garlic   1 sprig of fresh rosemary

4 large juicy tomatoes   2 tbsp olive oil

1 kg/2 lb new potatoes, scrubbed

Method

Put the oil into a roasting pan with a lid, an old fashioned oval roaster is fine or a large casserole will do. Heat it and brown the lamb all over in the oil for 2–3 minutes. Surround it with the potatoes, cut the peeled garlic into quarters and add that. Cut the tomatoes (which can be skinned if you are a purist) into quarters as well and add them. Season generously and place the rosemary sprig on top of the lamb. Cover and put in a very hot 425°F/220°C/200°C Fan/Gas Mark 7 roasting oven, using the top of the Aga roasting oven if you have one. Let it cook for about an hour turning the lamb (and the potatoes) once at least during this time. It should be brown and cooked through, this is not a pink lamb dish. When it's cooked the lamb should be almost falling off the bone, the tomatoes, garlic and juices should form a very little sauce and the potatoes should be beautifully browned. Serve the lamb in large pieces with some sauce poured over it and the potatoes alongside. Any other vegetables should be kept to another course.

< 179 >

ABBACCHIO ALLA CACCIATORA

This is lamb stew for the shoulder or other less luxurious cuts than leg of baby lamb. It's an unusual mixture of flavours but works very well. It's nice with mashed potatoes although I've never eaten it like that in Rome, where egg pasta, often in very large flat ribbon noodles, is much more commonly an accompaniment. Once again, even if you can't buy baby lamb in this country, fresh early British lamb works pretty well.

Ingredients

1 kg/2 lb lamb off the bone, cut into pieces the size of a walnut
2 tbsp olive oil
2 tbsp red wine vinegar
1 clove of garlic
1 sprig each of sage and rosemary
300 ml/½ pint of chicken stock or water

Method

Fry the pieces of lamb in the olive oil in a heatproof casserole until they are well browned. Add the clove of garlic, whole but lightly crushed, and deglaze the pan with the wine vinegar, stirring it round until it's almost vanished. Add the sage and rosemary and the stock or water. Stir the whole mixture together thoroughly, and simmer gently on the top of the stove or in a medium, 350°F/180°C/160°C Fan/Gas Mark 4/simmering oven of the Aga oven, for about an hour until the lamb is completely cooked and the sauce is much reduced to a delicious syrup.

HOT PANETONNE PUDDING

Though this seems like bread and butter pudding made with Italian cake, it's really quite authentic and may make bread and butter pudding redundant. Panetonne can be bought at any specialist grocers and many supermarkets around Easter. It's like a large, light fruit cake.

Serves 4.

< 180 >

Ingredients

50 g/2 oz butter plus extra for greasing
125 g/5 oz panetonne, torn into chunks
300 ml/½ pint milk

50 g/2 oz raisins
50 g/2 oz caster sugar
2 eggs

Pouring cream to serve (optional)

Method

Preheat the oven to 350°F/180°C/160°C Fan/Gas Mark 4/bottom of an Aga roasting oven. Scatter the raisins in the bottom of a buttered baking dish. Melt the butter in a pan and fry the panetonne for 3–4 minutes until golden, stirring constantly. Pour the contents of the pan in on top of the raisins. Beat the sugar, milk and eggs in a bowl and pour over the mixture through a sieve. The liquid should come to just below the very top of the bread. Bake for 25–30 minutes until golden brown and set. You can use a bain-marie to prevent the custard going grainy. Serve warm with a little cream.

< 181 >

Naples docks

< 182 >

NAPLES, CALABRIA, BASILICATA & CAMPAGNA

aples and the south-west of Italy, the bits that make up the ankle, instep and toe of the great Italian boot, have always been a place apart. In the years before Rome arose, Etruria was the great power in the north. The south was colonized by Greeks, bringing with them their culture, trade, language and wealth. From 500 BC onwards the whole southern coastline was peppered with Greek colonies, cities and trading posts. Many of the places that Homer wrote about in the *Odyssey* were in fact along this coast. First the Romans, then the Normans and last the Spanish ruled the area until the coming of the Italian Republic at the end of the nineteenth century. Now it's thought of as the poorest region of Italy.

In fact anyone who has ever visited Naples will be astonished to think that this, the most crowded and bustling city in Europe, has a single indolent citizen, but it is a land of vivid contrasts. The great city of Naples itself is enormously sophisticated. The largest opera house in Italy, built in the eighteenth century, nestles next to the oldest music conservatoire in Europe. Great churches, fine buildings and statues, some of them going back to the Greek period, adorn what is widely thought of as the most beautiful city in the Mediterranean. To perceive that beauty it's probably best to visit one of the headlands around the Bay of Naples and look across, as close to Naples has its grim and sordid side as well. But the area around abounds with cities, towns, coastlines and islands famous for their beauty. Capri and the Sorento Peninsula that leads to it, Amalfi and its famous coastline, Positano, possibly the most painted and photographed of all Italian fishing ports, are just some of the beauties that await the visitor.

Inland however matters are very different. Away from the smoky threat of Vesuvius the country becomes rapidly mountainous and in some places even forbidding. The beauty is undeniable, but Basilicata, the Campagna, and Calabria are hard country: the mountains and forests often plunging directly into the sea. It's nevertheless a major producer of marvellous raw materials and superb food. The area around Naples itself is extremely fertile thanks to the volcanic nature of the soil, and it's one of the great tomato and vegetable producing areas of the whole of the Italian peninsula. It's also famous for its cheeses, particularly mozzarella, pecorino made from sheep's milk, caprini, which are little goats cheeses often flavoured with herbs and provolone, a cow's milk cheese with a chewy texture.

< 183 >

Fruits grow well here too, particularly melons and peaches, and of course the sea has always been a great source. 'Blue' fish, anchovies and sardines are plentiful, but when you shop or eat out in Naples, or its surrounding countryside, remember that the most expensive thing you'll find on the menu will be fish. The only exceptions can be down in Calabria, where on the south coast large catches of tuna and swordfish are still brought ashore with great regularity. As far as meat goes, not much is eaten. As in all of Italy, pork is usually turned into preserved products like sausages, hams and salamis. The little meat that is eaten fresh tends to be lamb or goat.

The two dominant traditions in the cooking of this region are pasta and pizza. Pizza is often eaten as a kind of mobile breakfast in Naples. Circles of very thin dough, very lightly spread with fillings, are bought from stalls in the street early in the morning, the stalls usually fronting a restaurant that later in the day will serve the food more conventionally. They're folded in half to keep the filling in and are, I suspect, the origin of the calzone or closed pizza pie that's also a prominent part of the local cuisine. As far as pasta is concerned the people of the area are known as 'mangia maccheroni' or pasta eaters. It is the basic food of the majority of the population, eaten at least twice a day with a variety of very simple sauces. But this is plain pasta, no eggs or spinach or fancy colourings here. It's made from just water and hard (durum) wheat, sometimes with a little salt. The area became the first great manufacturer of pasta for sale and export in the nineteenth century, and those characteristic dark blue tubes of spaghetti had their origin in factories on the edge of Naples. The pasta in this part of the world is cooked *al dente*, with a little bite still left in the middle. It's never greased with butter but always with olive oil, and often moistened with a little drop or two of the water in which it was cooked.

The sauces too can be extremely simple, with garlic, a little oil and some herbs often being all that's added. Cheese often plays a part, and the very simple tomato sauces of the region are added too. Perhaps the most sophisticated of all the pasta dishes is the ragù, where rolls of meat stuffed with herbs and cheese are cooked gently for hours in a rich tomato sauce. This is eaten first with the appropriate pasta, the meat rolls being eaten subsequently with potatoes and vegetables. Pasta is often included in dishes which would seem strange anywhere else. It's baked in pies, and layered into timbales with vegetables. Vegetables indeed tend to dominate the cooking here with home-made pasta in varying forms eaten alongside the dried hard versions that are bought by all families. In the far south, in Basilicata, chillies also play an important part in the cooking, finding their way into everything from salads to seasoning oil, and often being combined, as in Abruzzi away to the north east, with lamb in stews and roasts.

Outside Naples, which is famous for its pastry shops and Easter cakes, there is little in the way of puddings eaten except of course for the famous *gelati*, and the various kinds of sorbets often called *granita* in this part of the world. As with the fanciful pastry confections, these are probably an inheritance from the Arab influence that swept through this part of the world when Sicily, just across the straits, was an Arab kingdom.

< 184 >

Bay of Naples

< 185 >

EATING OUT

In this part of the world eating out has more than one meaning, as many of the best restaurants have gardens and terraces or places where for most of the year you can eat in the open air, often amongst fruit trees and flowering groves. It's an opportunity not to be missed. Even the smallest trattoria often have tables on the pavements in a square, often even in a side-street where the traffic's fairly light. And certainly, if you can manage to get to one of the many beauty spots in the area, the peninsula of Sorento, the island of Capri or Ischia, or even one of the restaurants perched on the hills above Naples itself, the view can be as stunning as the food. That very beauty however has led to some problems of its own. The area is unbelievably popular with tourists, both from the north of Italy and the north of Europe, as well as local people for whom eating out is a natural and regular pleasure. In some of the best restaurants prices can be formidably high, particularly if you're eating fish. This tends to be cooked extremely simply, despite its price, as the fish themselves are increasingly rare in this area. It is however worth seeking out one or two of the better fish restaurants (not always on the coast) to experience just how good really fresh, simply cooked fish can be.

Antipasti are a great speciality here and most restaurants, even the smallest and simplest, will have a range of both cold and hot dishes to offer. These are usually based on vegetables, often in the slightly sweet and sour sauce known as *scapece*. There are usually two shellfish salads and sea food fritters, if you're lucky, a complete *fritta di mare* with all kinds of small seafood delicacies dipped in batter or breadcrumbs and quick fried. The *zuppa di pesce* is often the most delicious and economic way of tasting the local fish.

Don't miss out a pasta course which can come in any one of myriad forms. The main courses will tend to be simpler, with some meat or chicken offered, but don't miss out, once again, on the vegetable dishes, often based on aubergines, zucchini (both in their fully grown form and as their flowers), artichokes or peppers, often cooked with mozzarella or one of the other cheaper cheeses of the area. The first courses are often so delicious and plentiful that it's important to remember that there are main courses to come too. Normally fruit is the main dessert, but one or two restaurants, particularly in the Campagna and near Naples, also serve some extremely luxurious pastries, often quite generously spiced and very sweet. They have a strong Middle Eastern characteristic, occasionally modified by the generous use of ricotta, the creamy curd-like cheese that's eaten in so many different ways in this part of Italy.

Small, inexpensive cafés and restaurants abound, mostly patronized by the local people, and usually a reasonably substantial distance from any marina or fashionable shopping street. Guides tell you not to seek these out in unknown neighbourhoods in Naples after dark, but a good taxi service exists and the driver's advice is often worth taking for finding some of the restaurants that specialize particularly in the more traditional cooking of the region. By the

< 186 >

way, you may find it quite difficult to find pizzas at lunchtime as they tend to be breakfast and evening food. If you're in the right part of old Naples do try one for breakfast one day walking down the street. You buy your pizza, fold it in half and eat it with the crisp dough forming a kind of super sandwich around the highly flavoured filling. It brings a whole new pleasure to any concept of fast food and has the added virtue of being in the great tradition of eating in the street, for which Naples has been famous for three hundred years.

Apricot ice p. 201

< 187 >

AVOCADO, TOMATO AND MOZZARELLA SALAD

This modern salad is supposed to represent the Italian flag and is always dressed with the bright green leaves of fresh basil which spike it. If you're going to keep it at all, squeeze a little lemon juice over the avocado, cover with cling film and put it in the fridge. Try and find the real mozzarella di bufala or buffalo milk mozzarella native to Naples which has a unique texture and flavour.

Serves 4 as a starter.

Ingredients

2 small ripe avocados
100 g/4 oz mozzarella, thinly sliced
½ tsp sugar
2 tbsp shredded fresh basil

4 ripe tomatoes, thinly sliced
2 tbsp red wine vinegar
6 tbsp olive oil
Salt and freshly ground black pepper

Method

Cut the avocados in half and twist each one to get out the stone. Peel the skin off carefully in long ribbons. Place each half cut face down and slice it almost through lengthways, leaving a hinge on the thin end. Put it on a plate and press down a little and you'll find it will fan out into an attractive shape. Layer the tomatoes with alternate slices of mozzarella in the space left on the plates by the avocado. To make the dressing, place the vinegar, sugar, oil and plenty of seasoning in a screw-topped jar and shake until well combined. Drizzle over the salads and scatter the basil on top.

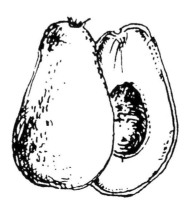

< **188** >

Saute di frutti di mare p. 191; avocado, tomato & mozzarella salad p. 188

< 189 >

PASTA MARGHERITA

This dish with its patriotic three colours of the Italian flag twice repeated in the pasta and the dressing, is named after Italy's first queen. The same sauce can be used with plain macaroni for equal flavour, though it's less spectacular.

Serves 4.

Ingredients

375 g/12 oz three-coloured spiral pasta shapes
2 tbsp olive oil
1 bunch spring onions, about 6
1 large red pepper, seeded and cut into 5 mm/¼ in strips
150 g/6 oz mozzarella cheese, cut into 5 mm/¼ in strips
Freshly grated parmesan, to garnish, optional
Fresh green salad, to serve

Method

Cook the pasta for 3–4 minutes in a large pan with plenty of boiling salted water and then remove from the heat. Cover with the lid, leave to stand for 7 minutes, then drain. Add half of the oil, toss thoroughly and set aside. Trim the spring onions, then chop the white and cut the green ends into 5 cm/2 in lengths. Heat the remaining olive oil in a frying pan and briskly fry the white part of the spring onions and the pepper for 3–4 minutes. Add four tablespoons of water and bring to the boil. Boil fast until all the water has evaporated and the vegetables are frying again. Add the cheese, the drained pasta and the remaining spring onion and turn together for 1–2 minutes until the mozzarella is heated through. Divide into wide-rimmed pasta bowls, sprinkle over a little parmesan, and serve with fresh green salad.

< 190 >

SAUTÉ DI FRUTTI DI MARE

A dish almost always eaten as a first course it uses whatever variety of fish happens to be to hand. It needs at least three different kinds of shellfish or sea food, which can, in Naples, vary from tiny octopus, so small that they're known as strawberries of the sea, up to large and substantial prawns or scampi. There's usually one kind of fish from the scampi family, one bivalve, such as clams or mussels, or even oysters, and some squid or octopus, if not in tiny form, cut up to suit the quick cooking method that's involved here. It's best served in small bowls or moderate sized plates which should have been warmed to start with, with plenty of good bread to mop up the juices.

Ingredients

150 g/6 oz raw shelled prawns or scampi (tiger prawns are fine for this)
2 dozen mussels or small clams, scrubbed and checked
225 g/8 oz cleaned squid (either tiny finger-sized or cut into 1 cm/½ in rings)

2 cloves of garlic	4 tbsp olive oil
1 lemon	2 tbsp chopped parsley

Method

Make sure the shellfish is well washed and free of any grit or sand. Heat the olive oil in a saucepan into which all the fish will go comfortably. A large frying pan is traditional in the area, but you may find a saucepan easier to handle for the first two or three goes. Finely chop the garlic and add that and the mussels or clams. Cover and shake the pan for 2 or 3 minutes until the shells open and the juices run out. Add the prawns and the squid. Season with salt and a little pepper and cook over a high heat until the prawns are pink and the squid is opaque. Add the finely chopped parsley and the lemon juice. Toss quickly and serve immediately into the warm bowls, making sure that everybody gets a portion of all three kinds of fish.

< 191 >

MACCHERONI AL POMODORO AL FORNO

Pasta is cooked in a lot of other ways in Campagna than simply boiling in water and serving with a sauce. It's used in bakes and pies and gratins. This is one of the nicest and simplest. I once saw Valentina Harris do a dish rather like this in a cookery demonstration in Britain and noticed that of all the dishes left backstage afterwards this one went the quickest. The sauce here is a modern version of the traditional Italian tomato sauce. It uses the small cherry tomatoes that are as prevalent in the south of Italy as they are in our supermarkets.

Ingredients

450 g/1 lb macaroni or penne (pasta with a hole in it)
675 g/1½ lb cherry tomatoes   2 tbsp olive oil
1 clove of garlic   1 bunch of spring onions
1 handful of fresh basil   2 tbsp grated parmesan
225 g/8 oz each of mozzarella and fontina cheese (450 g/1 lb of either will do)

Method

Bring a pan of water to the boil with a pinch of salt and a drop of oil, add the pasta and cook for 3–4 minutes. Cover, switch off the heat and leave for 7 minutes while you make the tomato sauce. Peel and chop the garlic, trim and finely chop the spring onions and cook in the olive oil for 2–3 minutes until golden. Add the cherry tomatoes, cut into quarters, season generously and simmer for 10 minutes. Cut the cheese or cheeses into 1 cm/½ in dice, drain the pasta, mix it with the tomato sauce and stir in the basil, finely chopped. Add the diced cheese, off the heat, and pour the mixture into a gratin dish. Sprinkle the top with the parmesan. It sometimes has some fresh breadcrumbs mixed with it, but should be a light, not a heavy, crusted coating. Bake in a medium oven, 350°F/180°C/170°C Fan/Gas Mark 4/bottom of Aga roasting oven for 20–30 minutes until bubbling and golden.

< 192 >

PIZZAS

Essential to any pizza is the base, and the recipe I give here creates a reasonably authentic copy of the Neapolitan style, thin and crispy pizza base. To cook it effectively you need a large and very hot oven, preferably made of brick. As these aren't readily available in most British kitchens, use a conventional oven heated up to close to its maximum temperature. If you're seeking real authenticity, a couple of tiles placed in it and heated up provide the kind of residual effect that the hot bricks provide in the authentic beehive-shaped oven. The dough is very easy to make and can be topped with a wide variety of fillings. Two or three are suggested here which have the virtue both of being authentic southern Italian and also containing no pineapple (as served in some American pizza houses).

Basic pizza dough makes 2 x 30 cm/12 in pizzas.

Ingredients

450 g/1 lb unbleached white bread flour
15 g/½ oz fresh yeast (or ½ sachet dried yeast)
Pinch of sugar (if using fresh yeast)

300 ml/½ pint warm water
4 tbsp olive oil
1 tsp salt

Method

Cream the fresh yeast and sugar together with a tablespoon or two of water from the measured quantity. Leave it aside for 10 minutes until it's frothy, mix the flour with the olive oil and the salt, until you get the effect of fine breadcrumbs. When the yeast is frothy stir it in (or add the dried yeast now) with the warm water. Mix together thoroughly and then knead by hand, in a food processor or in a kitchen mixer. By hand the kneading will take 4–5 minutes, about half that in a mixer, and about 1½ minutes in the processor. It should produce an elastic and coherent ball of dough whichever way you are mixing. Once it's firm and spongy coat it with a little more olive oil, put it in a bowl in a warm place covered with a tea towel, and leave it to rise for about 35–45 minutes. When it's doubled its size, knead it again for about 1 minute by hand. Divide it into two and spread it onto baking sheets or trays in the shape that you wish to make your pizza (it doesn't have to be round). It should stretch to not more than 1 cm/½ in thick and be even, except for the edges where you need to form a ridge with your finger and thumb all round. Top it with whatever toppings you've decided on (see recipes to follow) and allow it to rise for another 20 minutes or so with the toppings in place. Bake at 450°F/240°C/220°C Fan/Gas Mark 8/top of Aga roasting oven for 15–20 minutes depending on how thick your toppings are. If you're using tiles, place the baking tray directly onto those to get maximum heat to the bottom of the pizza, which should go crisp.

< 193 >

Pizzas pp. 195–6 (clockwise) Napolitana; garlic & herbs; Margherita; calzone p. 196

< 194 >

PIZZA WITH GARLIC AND HERBS

Ingredients

4 cloves of garlic

4 tbsp olive oil

1½ tbsp fresh or frozen oregano

1 tsp sea salt

Black pepper

Method

Spread the oil over the pastry – making sure it covers all but the edges. Chop the garlic very finely and spread evenly over the surface. Top with the herbs and finally with the sea salt. This will probably need less time to bake than any of the others.

NAPOLITANA

This is the traditional tomato based pizza.

Ingredients

2 tbsp tomato paste

4 tbsp olive oil

4 tbsp chopped Italian tomatoes (tinned)

1 clove of garlic, finely chopped

1 tsp each of fresh oregano and basil (or frozen or freeze dried)

Method

Mix the finely chopped garlic into the tomato paste and spread over the whole of the base of the pizza, avoiding the edges. Spread the chopped tomato over the top, sprinkle over the herbs, season generously and dribble the oil in a spiral from the edge.

DOUBLE MOZZARELLA

This is a speciality of the south of Italy. Try and use mozzarella di bufala if you can find it, as the flavour here is essentially based on the cheese.

Ingredients

1 clove of garlic

350 g/12 oz finely chopped or shredded mozzarella cheese

50 g/2 oz parmesan, grated

2 tbsp olive oil

1 tsp salt

1 tsp oregano

Method

Crush the garlic with the salt and spread it on the pizza base, avoiding the edges. Pile the grated or shredded mozzarella across the surface of the pizza. Sprinkle the parmesan, olive oil and the oregano. Bake in the hottest of ovens, watching occasionally after 15 minutes for the cheese to be bubbling and with golden flakes, but not burning in any area.

< 195 >

PIZZA MARGHERITA

This pizza is often added to with one or two small but savoury ingredients like a tin of anchovies or 6 or 7 chopped capers to increase the piquancy. I'm an anchovy man myself but it's very good without either of them, if you prefer, in the more authentic version.

Ingredients

6 oz Italian chopped tinned tomatoes

6 oz grated or shredded mozzarella

4 tbsp olive oil

A handful of basil

1 clove of garlic

1 tsp salt

Method

Crush the garlic with the salt and spread it on the pizza base. Top it with the tomatoes. Sprinkle on the cheese, not worrying too much if it's not a perfectly even coating. Rough chop the basil, add that and dribble the olive oil over the top before baking. This pizza will take longer than most. If you are adding anchovies or capers, add those just before you drizzle over the olive oil. Some people use the oil from the anchovy tin to add that flavour to the whole pizza, in which case it's sometimes called Pizza Marinara.

CALZONE

These are, to look at, the Italian equivalent of Cornish pasties, but in fact they're pizzas folded over and sealed before being baked. They can contain a wide variety of ingredients, as can pizzas themselves. This version, which uses ricotta, comes from the tip of Calabria near Sicily where ricotta is often used in tarts and pies.

Ingredients

1 x 30 cm/12 in pizza dough portion

12 stoned black olives

225 g/8 oz ricotta cheese

1 tin anchovies, drained of oil

6 tbsp Italian chopped tinned tomatoes, drained of their liquid

Method

Chop the anchovies and halve the olives. Mix those into the ricotta and stir in the drained tomato pieces. A light sprinkling of oregano or basil can be added at this stage. Roll out the dough once it has risen and been kneaded the second time, to a 30 cm/12 in circle without raised edges. Place the filling in half the disc, leaving an inch of space around the edge. Fold the other half over and pinch shut, rolling the edge up all the way round to act as a double seal. Place on a greased baking sheet in a maximum heat 450°F/240°C/220°C Fan/Gas Mark 8/top of Aga roasting oven and bake for 20–25 minutes until the dough is golden brown. They are traditionally eaten hot, but although they are theoretically finger food, I find it easier to eat them on a plate.

< 196 >

AUBERGINES PARMIGIANA

There are many different versions of this dish, not only in the south, but now all over Italy. But aubergines, undoubtedly, are at their most popular in the area around, and to the south of Naples. This makes a really substantial dish which, although often eaten as a side dish or a first course, I think makes a perfect vegetarian main course. I eat it on its own with plenty of bread followed by a salad and perhaps preceded by a fairly light pasta dish without tomatoes or cheese.

Ingredients

675 g/1½ lb aubergines
1 tin of Italian tomatoes
1 medium onion
1 clove of garlic
1 tsp each of oregano and basil
½ tsp sugar
350 g/12 oz mozzarella, in slices
75 g/3 oz parmesan
4 tbsp olive oil

Method

Slice the aubergines into 5 mm/¼ in thick slices lengthwise. Traditionally they were then salted and left for the bitter juices to run out, but modern aubergines don't much need that. You can salt them lightly, if you like, while making the tomato sauce, heating a tablespoon of the oil in the saucepan, adding the chopped garlic and the tinned tomatoes, the sugar and the oregano. Simmer for 15–20 minutes. If you've salted the aubergines, wash them carefully. Heat the remaining olive oil in a frying pan, and sauté the aubergine slices briefly in this. You may need to add a little more oil as aubergine does absorb a lot as it fries. In a gratin dish, put a layer of aubergine, a third of the tomato sauce, a layer of Mozzarella slices, and repeat twice more. The individual layers should be quite thin. Sprinkle the basil over the top and add the parmesan. Bake in a medium oven, 350°F/180°C/170°C Fan/Gas Mark 4/bottom of Aga roasting oven for about 30–35 minutes until bubbling and golden.

< 197 >

ZUCCHINI

Zucchini, or baby marrows, are universal throughout all the three provinces of the south-west. They're eaten in all kinds of forms: in salads, both fresh and cooked, as an ingredient in mixed vegetable dishes, as an alternative to aubergines in a wide range of baked and layered food, in fritters, stuffed and, not least, baby ones attached to their bright orange yellow flowers in a variety of spectacular presentations. This is a simple but unusually flavoured dish which makes particularly nice individual presentation.

ZUCCHINI E UOAVA

Ingredients

450 g/1 lb zucchini (courgettes)
50 g/2 oz grated parmesan
2 tbsp olive oil

4 eggs
Small sprig of rosemary
1 tbsp butter

Method

When buying the courgettes, look for the smallest, shiniest vegetables you can find. Wash them, top and tail them, and cut them into lengthwise strips, rather like triangular chips, about 50 mm/2 in long. If the courgettes are big, cut each chip in half again lengthwise. Sauté them gently in the olive oil until they are wilted but not cooked right through, this should take about 3–4 minutes. Strip the leaves off the sprig of rosemary and add that to the courgettes as they cook. Beat the eggs in a bowl and add half the parmesan. In a separate, preferably non-stick pan, scramble the eggs in the butter until they are still runny but starting to set. Stir in the zucchini and divide into four equal portions in small gratin or mini soufflé dishes. Smooth down the top, sprinkle over the rest of the parmesan and put under a hot grill for 2–3 minutes until the parmesan is melted and the top is bubbling. Serve immediately as a separate first course or to go with simple plain meats.

< 198 >

STEAK PIZZAEOLA

This comes from the most remote part of southern Italy, off the normal tourist routes. A pizza cook must have come there and put his pizza sauce on a steak! One of the great benefits of a sauce like this is that you can use slightly smaller steaks. It also goes well with lamb in leg steaks or fillets. Lamb, particularly in the hills, is a much favoured meat in Basilicata – still a land of shepherds.

Ingredients

4 x 175 g/6 oz sirloin or rump steaks
1 tbsp pesto sauce
Salt and freshly ground black pepper

100 g/4 oz can chopped tomatoes
1 garlic clove, finely chopped
Few drops of chilli sauce

Soft Italian noodles and green salad, to serve

Method

Heat the grill for at least five minutes before putting on the steaks. Mix together the tomatoes, pesto sauce, garlic and chilli sauce. When the grill is really hot, cook the steaks for two minutes on one side. Now season the steaks, turn them over and spread a quarter of the mixture on each of them. Return the steaks to the grill and cook for another two minutes for rare, three minutes for medium and four minutes for ruined! Serve at once with the noodles. Other vegetables should be separate courses.

< 199 >

TARTA DI RICOTTA

There are a number of versions of this pastry enclosed cheesecake made in the Neapolitan region. It's flavoured in a variety of ways too, with everything from *strega*, the yellow liqueur named after witches, through to the simpler and, to my taste, rather more pleasant flavours of citrus fruits. This calls for a substantial quantity of ricotta, the Italian equivalent of cottage cheese; British ricotta tends to be more liquid than the Italian version, and I follow Marcella Hazan, introducing a way of getting rid of some of the liquid in the ricotta before attempting to make the tart, which otherwise can come out a bit soggy. I suggest you use shortcrust pastry for this. Very often in Italy they make a sweet pastry that's extremely sweet, something like 2–3 oz sugar to 8 oz flour, which I find overwhelms the pie. If you make your own shortcrust, you may care to add half a tablespoon of icing sugar to the mixture. If you're buying shortcrust, I'd just leave it at that.

Ingredients

Filling

800 g/1¾ lb ricotta   15 g /½ oz butter
100 g/ 4 oz mixed peel   3 eggs
2 tbsp caster sugar   550 g/1¼ lb short crust pastry
Grated rind of 1 lemon and 1 orange and the juice of half of each

Method

To prepare the ricotta, put it into a saucepan, preferably non-stick, and heat up over a medium heat, stirring gently from time to time. You'll find that it separates and quite a lot of liquid runs out. When you've cooked it for about 10–12 minutes, line a colander with a piece of muslin or, failing that, a piece of kitchen paper, and tip the mixture from the pan in, allowing the liquid to run away into a bowl or into the sink. Stir it a little and leave it in the colander until the ricotta mixture ceases to drip. Put it in a bowl, separate the eggs and add the mixed peel, the sugar, the grated rind and juices of the lemon and orange and the egg yolks. Mix thoroughly and leave to stand while you roll out the pastry in two rounds, one containing two-thirds and one containing one-third. Grease a 20 cm/8 in spring form cake tin and, use the larger circle of pastry to line the tin, leaving a little proud at the top. Whip the egg whites and mix those gently into the ricotta and fruit mixture, being careful not to squash all the air out of the egg whites again. Put into the pastry shell and cover with the smaller circle of pastry. Crimp the edges using your fingers. Traditionally this is crimped so that the edges stand up

< 200 >

straight, rather like a small battlement around the pie. Brush the top of the cake with a little of the egg mixture or some milk, and bake in a medium oven, 350°F/180°C/170°C Fan/Gas Mark 4/bottom of the Aga roasting oven for 55 minutes. The cake should be bright gold and the pastry cooked through but not dark brown. Remove from the oven and put it on a rack for 5 minutes or so until you can remove the sides of the tin. Allow it to cool on its base completely for at least 12 hours before serving. Refrigeration isn't necessary and doesn't improve the flavour or texture, in fact it often just makes the pastry very soggy. It doesn't need much addition this, though I have eaten it with a small salad of very ripe oranges as an accompaniment.

APRICOT ICE

In the deep south of Italy fruit abounds, fruit of all sorts but one of the earliest to have been cultivated was the apricot. It was the favourite of the Arabs who were rulers of Sicily and, for a while, of parts of the mainland. In this recipe they are used in a simple version of that old favourite of the Arabs – water ice or sherbet. You can use canned fruit in its own juice in which case start the recipe after the apricot halves have been cooked.

Serves 4.

Ingredients

675 g/1½ lb apricots
125 g/5 oz caster sugar

1 cinnamon stick
Crisp lemon biscuits, to serve

Method

Dip the apricots into a bowl of boiling water for 30 seconds. Then slip the skins off and cut each one in half to remove the stones. Place the apricot halves in a pan with 300 ml/½ pint of water and the cinnamon stick. Simmer for 15 minutes until the apricots are just tender. Drain, reserving 150 ml/¼ pint of the cooking water and liquidize to a purée. Return the reserved cooking water to the pan and add the sugar. Heat gently to dissolve and remove from the heat. Stir in the apricot purée and pour into a rigid plastic container. Freeze for at least 4 hours. Just before you are ready to serve, place the apricot mixture in the food processor or liquidizer and process to a thick mush. Spoon into tall glasses and serve at once with the biscuits.

< 201 >

Old harbour at Bari

< **202** >

APULIA

Apulia is a region that's had the most extraordinary changes of fortune. As far back as the eighth century BC, it was a hugely important part of the expanding empire of the Greek cities. In this case Sparta was the leader here, and indeed some of the food and other traditions are believed to go back to that distant time. The Greek influence is so strong that some of the towns still have Greek names, and in two or three of them a dialect is spoken called Greki, more easily understood by the citizens of Athens than of Rome.

Of all the south Puglia is the economic success. This follows partly from the physical circumstances of the country. Unlike the rest of the south of Italy the 'high heel', which the province forms, has vast fertile plains and its agricultural produce is considerable. Most of the olive oil and most of the wine that Italy produces comes from this region. There's industry too, both manufacturing and lighter industry such as clothing, and the Eastern connection with Brindisi and Bari – the ports that have greatest access to the Eastern Mediterranean acting as focuses for both trade and cosmopolitan interests. Although it bustles once more Apulia retains a lot of very old-fashioned attitudes along with its extraordinary architecture. There are peasant buildings called 'Trulli' in parts of the region. No one knows the exact origin of these dome-like buildings but it was a cheap way to build. It developed its own version of both Romanesque and Baroque, and its food too can be most distinctive. It's perhaps most famous for its hand-made pasta, particularly the Orecchiette, or little ears of pasta. You can buy these in shops but the tradition is that they were hand-made and the very shape was created by the thumbprint of the woman making them. They are eaten with a variety of different sauces, some quite distinctive to the region like the Orecchiette con Rapini, or pasta with turnip tops and anchovies. Most of the other pasta in this area is very different from the long style eaten on the other side of Italy around Naples. It's almost always small and short, usually quite fat, takes a little longer to cook, and has a variety of extraordinary names as well which are almost impossible to list, though the very names themselves have an attraction – Pestazzule or Stacchiotte.

There is a strong tradition in Apulia too of preserves. Indeed, they preserve almost anything, starting of course with tomatoes, which are preserved in such a wide variety of ways as to make them almost different vegetables. Tiny ones are hung up in bunches and somehow or other, right the way through the winter, manage to remain sweet and full of juice. They also make a variety of tomato pulps, sometimes raw

< 203 >

and sometimes cooked down. There are salted whole tomatoes and sliced and puréed ones, sometimes they are washed in vinegar, preserved in olive oil with chillies, sometimes they're sandwiched round grated cheese. Aubergines, mushrooms and artichokes are also preserved and there is the usual range of salted and pickled meats and salamis. Figs are preserved in honey, olives are brined, fish is salted, and fruit is often preserved in various forms of alcohol.

There is also a habit of eating some of the excellent cheeses as part of a first course, a very unusual pattern in Italy. Particularly popular are their versions of fresh mozzarella and ricotta. The mozzarella tends to come in small marble-sized balls, eaten within a day or so of being made. Sometimes it's plaited in thin strands and then sliced across to produce an extraordinary mosaic pattern. One version of ricotta also includes a couple of fermented versions which have a much stronger and richer flavour.

All kinds of fish are eaten and tuna and red mullet are great favourites. Fish stews and soups feature widely and so also does a particularly delicious way of grilling a variety of fish – a low fat version of the Fritto Misto called the Grigliata Mista. They are fond of skewers in Puglia and often you'll find a variety of shellfish, fish, meat or even vegetables marinated in the local olive oil and lemon juice, and then grilled or occasionally oven baked before being served very simply.

Puddings don't put in much of an appearance. More likely is a large plate of the extraordinarily good fruit, and particularly water melon, that the region specializes in. There is also an older tradition of serving certain 'digestive' vegetables at the end of a meal, much as we might eat a piece of fruit, with fennel and some very tender celery figuring in the plate that's offered. There is a range of ice-creams, usually made with some of the local fruit. The Arab influence also leads to the ready use of almonds and honey in occasional pastries and tarts, though these aren't nearly as widespread as they are in Sicily and Naples.

Last but not least, it's important to mention Apulian bread. It's probably the most interesting bread that's baked in Italy, *ciabatta* notwithstanding. This is partly because of the use of a variety of flours; it's the only place in Italy where you regularly get wholemeal bread. They make huge loaves large enough to feed a family for a couple of days, with superb crusts, and there are also speciality breads, particularly flavoured regionally with tomatoes and garlic or black olives or fennel seeds. Sometimes they're quite small, from the *turallini* breadsticks, which are often dipped in water or wine at the beginning of a meal, to the much larger *friselle* which are used even now by fishermen, who have been known to dip them in the sea to get the water and salt that make them particularly palatable at the same time.

< **204** >

Trulli at Albero Bello

< **205** >

EATING OUT

With the exception of the two or three large towns, Lecce, Brindisi and Bari, most eating out in Apulia is of necessity done in small and very individual restaurants. Some of them specialize in dishes derived from historical food treatises written by the rulers of the region or their famous chefs. Even these restaurants though make a point of supplying the specialities of the region. Very few of them will be unwise enough to offer a menu that didn't include Orecchiette, and at least one dish in which broad beans played a significant part.

On the coast fish is still king and, unlike most parts of Italy, at a reasonable price. Look for the Zuppa di Pesci, very often not made with tomatoes in this region. Dishes of mussels and rice, the Fritto Misto or Grigliata Mista will almost certainly include red mullet and the local scampi, and may well include some of the tiny fish rather like our whitebait marinated in a sweet and sour sauce. Main courses containing meat may be unusual in that lamb and horse meat are likely to be central to the matter at hand. There are some unusual lamb sausages which are called by the wonderful name *Gnemeriedde*. While very tasty it's probably better not to enquire too closely about the contents.

Inland, a number of the *masseria*, ancient fortified farmhouses, have been turned into restaurants. Here, as elsewhere in Apulia, the *antipasti* are really the star of the show. Main courses are simple and grilled, with vegetables often taking centre stage and, as so often in the area, puddings will tend to be either a range of fruit (don't miss the prickly pears and figs if they're available) with a few simple fruit tarts added to the list of ice-creams for a little variety. It's worth asking at these sort of establishments, what the owners or managers, usually the same thing, recommend both seasonally and in terms of their own specialities. In Apulia the unexpected is usually available and often quite delicious.

< 206 >

IL CRUDO

Although literally translated this fish dish means 'raw', actually it's more like the Mexican seviches than the Japanese sushi method of eating fish. All kinds of fish are eaten in this way, in Apulia, although it's always swimming fish rather than shellfish that are treated so. Occasionally the marinating in lemon juice, which effectively 'cooks' the fish, is cut to a minimum and the fish is eaten almost straight off the bone with the dressing added. I don't think it's nearly as nice that way as when the lemon juice has had a chance to turn it opaque and firm the flesh up a little bit. In Britain, probably the best fish to use to cook in this way are red mullet and sardines, (fresh – not from the tin), but other fish that's firm fleshed like monkfish or haddock will also respond very nicely in this direction. The rather exotic tilapia, which is now in many supermarkets and fish shops, also goes well. Choose the red rather than the black kind.

Ingredients

450 g/1 lb carefully filleted fish
6 tbsp olive oil
Juice of another lemon
Parsley or fennel

4 tbsp lemon juice
2 spring onions
½ tsp salt
Chilli pepper flakes

Method

Trim the fillets and cut them into 2.5 cm/1 in slices. Place them in a china or glass bowl and pour the lemon juice over them, turning them completely. Leave them to marinate for at least 4–6 hours in the fridge. The flesh will turn white as though they have been cooked on heat. Finely chop the spring onions. Add those and the salt to the juice of the extra lemon, adding chilli pepper flakes to taste. Start with about half a teaspoon and only add more if you feel you really need it. Whisk in the olive oil until the sauce is thickened. Remove the fish from the lemon juice marinade. Pour the dressing over the top, sprinkle with parsley or fennel, finely chopped, and serve cool.

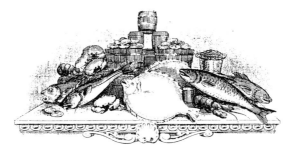

< 207 >

CIALLEDDA

This cold vegetable soup is unrelated but very similar to the Gazpacho made in Spain, but is rather simpler with the vegetables in bigger pieces. At the heart of it is the use of bread to make an almost porridge-like consistency. I like it a little thinner than that with the vegetables rather more varied than just the traditional onion, garlic and tomato, but the basic concept is wonderfully refreshing in hot weather, and also, when you have good vegetables, heightens their flavour most remarkably.

Ingredients

4 large vine ripened tomatoes
1 large Spanish type mild or sweet onion
900 ml/1½ pints water
1 heaped tsp salt

Half a cucumber
1 green pepper
6 tbsp olive oil
1 clove of garlic

4 slices rustic white bread (this can be old but not stale)

Method

Mix the oil and water together in a large bowl. Crush the peeled garlic with the salt and stir that in thoroughly. Rough chop the tomatoes, the seeded pepper and the peeled onion and add those to the mixture. Split the cucumber in half lengthwise, scoop out the seeds and rough chop the remaining flesh. Crumble the bread into the soup with your hands. Tradition is divided about whether or not to include the crusts. I tend to leave them out as they make the soup rather chewy. Stir the mixture together and leave it for at least half an hour in the fridge – it benefits from a couple of hours. At that moment, check it to see that the consistency is right. I like it about as thick as single cream. You may need to add a little more water or a little more bread to produce that balance. Serve it in bowls sprinkled, if you like, with fresh herbs – basil or parsley or even fresh oregano are quite delicious.

< 208 >

Pepperonatta with ricotta p. 210; cialledda p. 208

< **209** >

PEPPERONATTA WITH RICOTTA

This is a salad which, in its original form, requires a lot of complex grilling and peeling of the peppers. This is to get rid of the rather waxy outside coating but the crafty method here allows that same coating to be cooked off without too much fiddling about. The contrast between the sweetness of the peppers and the clear tasting creaminess of the ricotta makes this an outstanding first course.

Serves 4 as a starter.

Ingredients

675 g/1½ lb sweet peppers (mixed colours)
1 garlic clove, crushed
100 g/4 oz ricotta

2 tbsp olive oil
Juice of 1 lemon
1 tbsp chopped fresh parsley

Salt and freshly ground black pepper

Method

Halve the peppers, remove the seeds and slice across into 5 mm/¼ in strips. Heat the oil in a frying pan which will take all the peppers. Add the garlic and then immediately add the pepper slices. Cook over a high heat for 2–3 minutes, stirring constantly. Season well, reduce the heat and leave the peppers to cook gently for about 10 minutes until they are just beginning to caramelize. Sprinkle over the lemon juice, turn thoroughly and leave to cool completely. To serve, divide the pepper mixture among four plates and spoon some of the ricotta into a ball in the centre of each plate. Sprinkle over the parsley.

ORECCHIETTE WITH RAPE

This is really a very ancient Pugliese dish. Orecchiette, or little ears, are the traditional hand-made pasta of the region and are to be found everywhere both hand-made still and manufactured. You can find them in supermarkets specializing in Italian (as opposed to British copies of Italian) pasta. But even in Apulia similar small pasta of different shapes is

< 210 >

Orecchiette with rape p. 210

< 211 >

often used. *Cavatelli*, little curled fingers of macaroni, or *conghille*, the pasta that looks like snails, can quite reasonably be substituted. There's a little trouble with the rape as well. Literally translated it means 'turnip tops' but they're not our turnips, rather more resembling the very thin broccoli sprigs that we get sometimes in this country, known as purple sprouting broccoli, with thin stems, a slightly knobbly head and some leaf attached. It can be made with the large mountainous green heads that seem prevalent everywhere these days, but if you can find purple sprouting it's very much closer to the original form. This is a country dish with lots of flavour and very easy to make.

Ingredients

450 g/1 lb orecchiette or cavatelli pasta
450 g/1 lb broccoli or broccoli spear florets
100 g/4 oz parmesan cheese

2 cloves of garlic
100 ml/4 fl oz olive oil
Half a tin of anchovies

Method

Trim the broccoli florets. If you're using the large-headed types, cut them into 10 mm/½ in florets. Bring a large saucepan of water to the boil, add salt and a teaspoon of oil and add the pasta, stirring it for a moment. Cook for 3 minutes and add the broccoli florets. Cook for 6–8 minutes until the pasta is cooked through and the broccoli is still green. Meanwhile, in another reasonably large saucepan, put the oil with the finely chopped garlic and the anchovies with their oil. Cook gently, mashing the anchovies until they dissolve into the oil and garlic mixture. Be careful not to let either of them brown. Drain the pasta and broccoli quickly but not too thoroughly, and stir into the saucepan with the oil mixture, turning them thoroughly over a low heat until completely coated. Check for seasoning and serve with lots of black pepper and the parmesan cheese to sprinkle over.

PENNE CON ZUCCHINI

This is a most delicious pasta and courgette dish, easy and very quick to cook, inexpensive and pretty kind to the waistline! Penne, or quills, are bits of pasta about 5 cm/2 in long which are hollow with pointed ends. They actually look a little like a large macaroni, but the insides

< 212 >

are ridged to hold the sauce. The use of yoghurt, it must be said, is not authentic but works very well and in some ways resembles the Pugliese use of fermented ricotta.

Serves 4.

Ingredients

350 g/12 oz penne or similar pasta shapes

350 g/12 oz courgettes, coarsely grated

250 ml/8 fl oz natural thick Greek yoghurt

2 tbsp olive oil

1 heaped tsp cornflour

A few fresh basil leaves, torn

Salt and freshly ground black pepper

Method

Cook the pasta in a large pan of boiling salted water for 4 minutes and remove from the heat. Cover and set aside for 7–8 minutes until the pasta is just al dente. Drain well. Heat the oil in a large frying pan, add the courgettes and cook for about 2 minutes until they are really hot, stirring occasionally. Stir the cornflour into the yoghurt – this stops it separating when it is heated – and pour into the pan. Stir it carefully until it is really hot, do not boil. Place the penne in a warmed serving bowl and spoon over the courgette sauce. Scatter over the basil and serve.

AUBERGINES WITH HERBS

As with so many parts of Italy, particularly in the south where the Arab influence was considerable, aubergines are a fundamental part of the cooking. This is a very simple recipe for grilled aubergines with lots of herbs. The use of mint is unusual but again has its roots in the Arab tradition. In the old days aubergines used to be sliced and salted extensively to get rid of the bitter juices, but currently the aubergines we buy in Britain don't seem to need this activity. If you feel like salting them first, do. Make sure you rinse them thoroughly.

< 213 >

Ingredients

900 g/2 lb aubergines, with black glossy skins   **150 ml/¼ pint olive oil**
6 cloves of garlic, peeled and finely chopped
½ tbsp each of fresh oregano and mint and basil
2 dsp Aceto Vechio (balsamic vinegar is an adequate substitute)

Method

Remove the green caps from the aubergines and slice them lengthwise about a quarter to a third of an inch thick. Brush them with the olive oil, sprinkle with the garlic and grill them on a hot grill (a barbecue is fine for this if you like it) for about 4–5 minutes a side until they are well browned on both sides. Put them on a large plate and sprinkle them with the vinegar and then the finely chopped herbs. Pour the remaining oil over the aubergines using a spiral motion to make sure as much of them as possible are covered. Leave to marinate for three hours. Turn, making sure that some of the herbs reach both sides of the aubergines, and marinate for another three hours, up to twelve is fine. To serve, arrange neatly on the plate and sprinkle a little fresh basil or parsley over the top for a bright green colour.

BROAD BEAN AND ARTICHOKE CASSEROLE

There are wide numbers of recipes for this local favourite which has enthusiasts over the border in Basilicata and Campagna as well. While the basic recipes are all similar, details vary quite a lot, some including ham or bacon, some potatoes, some made with dried broad beans and some with fresh, some even add peas. This is a simple version in assuming that you can buy both fresh broad beans and fresh artichokes. There's about a two month window in Britain when this is true. If not, the easiest thing is to buy either frozen broad beans or canned artichoke hearts (not in vinegar). I like the modifying effect of a little potato in the recipe as well as both the other ingredients are really strongly flavoured.

Ingredients

12 oz (podded) fresh broad beans
4 artichokes (or 4 artichoke hearts)
150 g/6 oz onion   **4 tbsp olive oil**
450 g/1 lb potatoes   **Salt and pepper**

< 214 >

Method

If you are using fresh artichokes, strip away all the leaves, cut the base flat and remove the hairy choke from the centre. This should leave you with a slightly concave dish about 5 cm/2 in across. If you are using tinned artichokes, drain them thoroughly and rinse in fresh cold water but don't add them until halfway through the cooking as they have already been poached in the tin. Peel the potatoes and peel and slice the onion. Put the oil in the pan into which all the vegetables will go comfortably and sauté the onion until it starts to go brown. Cut the artichoke hearts into quarters and the potatoes into 10 mm/½ in slices. Add those and stir them with the onion until they are coated with the oil. Add the broad beans and enough cold water just to cover. Season generously with salt and cook gently, stirring as little as possible but not allowing the vegetables to stick. You may need to add a little more water as you go. It should be cooked completely in about 15–20 minutes with very little liquid left in the bottom of the pan. Serve as a course in its own right or with grilled sausages or meat skewers. Plenty of black pepper over the top at the end is a very good idea.

MEDITERRANEAN VEGETABLE SKEWERS

Cooking on skewers is a speciality of Apulia, perhaps reflecting the Greek connection. As vegetables are also a local passion, it is inevitable that the two should meet. It is this kind of cooking that has led American and Northern European nutritionists to enthuse so much about the 'Mediterranean diet'. Vegetables, olive oil and grilling all rolled into one.

Serves 4.

Ingredients

1 small aubergine
1 red onion
2 tbsp olive oil
1 tsp clear honey
100 g/4 oz cherry tomatoes

1 yellow pepper
1 courgette
1 tbsp fresh lemon juice
1 tbsp chopped fresh oregano
Salt and freshly ground black pepper

< 215 >

Aubergines with herbs p. 213; Mediterranean vegetable skewers p. 215; grigliata mista p. 217

< 216 >

Method

Cut the aubergine into 2.5 cm/1 in pieces. Cut the pepper in half, remove the seeds and cut each half into six pieces. Peel the onion, leaving the root intact, and cut into eight wedges. Trim the courgette and cut into 2.5 cm/1 in pieces. Preheat the grill. Mix together the olive oil, lemon juice, honey, oregano and seasoning and place in a large bowl. Add all the prepared vegetables with the tomatoes and toss to coat. Thread on to eight wooden skewers that have been soaked in water for 30 minutes, to prevent them from burning. Place on to the grill rack and brush with any remaining oil. Grill for 10–15 minutes, turning and brushing frequently until the vegetables are lightly charred. Serve immediately.

GRIGLIATA MISTA

This is a version, not unique to Apulia but much practised there, of grilling the same sort of mixture of fish and seafood that you would expect to find in a *fritto misto*, the deep fried version of the dish. As always in these matters, the fish you can easily obtain are the ones that are normally served, but the selection of fish easily obtained along the Bari coast is usually rather more exiting than that in our normal fishmongers, so you may need a little planning to achieve this. The best trick is to aim at not more than four kinds of fish and to make sure that there is some quite substantial pieces, probably tuna or monkfish or swordfish, all of which are easily obtainable in Britain now, as the basis and add the more expensive speciality ingredients like lobster or large prawns in smaller quantities. This is probably best done on a barbecue grill, though it is equally possible to achieve the same effect, though not the same dramatic cooking presentation, on a domestic grill providing you get it really hot. The problem there, probably, is cooking enough at a time to feed more than three or four people.

Serves 6.

Ingredients

900 g/2 lb fish steaks, tuna, swordfish, monkfish or cod
12 tiger prawns in their shells, heads removed
450 g/1 lb squid (6 small or 2 large)
1 clove of garlic
4 tbsp chopped fennel leaves

6 small red mullet
150 ml/¼ pint olive oil
Juice of 2 lemons
1 tsp salt
2 bay leaves

< 217 >

Method

Get your fishmonger to do the work for you, cleaning the mullet (they often leave the liver in which is considered a speciality) and cleaning the squid, but not cutting it into rings. Make a marinade whisking the lemon juice, the garlic crushed with the salt, the finely chopped fennel, the bay leaves and the olive oil all together. Marinate the fish in this for at least an hour, up to 6 hours in the fridge is fine. If the squid comes in one or two large pieces, cut it into postcard-sized strips. Preheat your grill or get your barbecue to the maximum grilling temperature. Brush the grill itself lightly with oil, a piece of kitchen paper is a good idea for this, wadded up. Place the fish on in the order that it needs cooking. The fish steaks and the red mullet should go on first and will probably need 4–5 minutes a side. When you have turned those for the first time, add the squid and the prawns and grill those, turning them so that they have 2½–3 minutes a side. Make sure the fish is cooked through but not at all dried out. Serve it on a large spectacular platter with more lemon cut into quarters, plenty of chopped parsley to go over the top and maybe even a little of the marinade that's left, heated in a small saucepan on the side of the barbecue or on your stove, and use to brush over the fish steaks just before you serve them. Anything but lots and lots of fresh crusty bread would be a mistake. Serve salads and vegetables separately.

TUNA IN SPICY TOMATO SAUCE

A very simple fisherman style dish this, reminiscent of all kinds of rustic seaside cookery. It's not a sauce or a technique confined to Apulia but is often to be found there; it's where they don't only cook tuna but also octopus and squid in this manner.

Ingredients

450 g/1 lb fresh tuna, cut into four pieces
450 g/1 lb fresh ripe tomatoes or a tin of chopped Italian tomatoes
2 cloves of garlic
1 medium sized onion
100 ml/4 fl oz olive oil
Pinch of sugar
Salt and pepper

< 218 >

Method

Make a tomato sauce, frying the finely chopped and peeled onion and garlic in the oil until lightly browned, adding the tomatoes (if they are fresh cut them into quarters) and simmering with a pinch of sugar and salt and pepper for 15–20 minutes until the sauce is well blended and reduced. At this point other flavourings are sometimes introduced, capers, anchovies and chillies, but I prefer it without. Add the tuna steaks, making sure that they are covered in the sauce. Turn the heat down low, put the lid on the pan and simmer gently for about 8–12 minutes until the tuna is cooked through and the sauce has reduced a little more. Serve it with small pasta. Although it's not conventional in Apulia, it's particularly good with well cooked long grain rice.

BRACIOLE AL RAGÙ

The tradition of stuffed meat rolls cooked in a rich tomato sauce and then eaten as two courses, the sauce with pasta and the meat with vegetables, is one that exists all over Italy, particularly in the south. If the rolls are small they are called '*involtini*' and I can remember eating them with a Sicilian friend decades ago where they were a revelation stuffed with garlic and parsley. Some versions have great rounds of meat which can be beef, pork or, in Apulia, traditionally horsemeat, stuffed with a mixture of cheese, herbs, and sometimes salamis as well. The method I give here is a little bit of a cheat but extremely authentic as it comes from my very good friend Antonio Carluccio, who says in his book 'Italian Cooking' that it was his mother's method of making this dish on a rather more economic scale. I've amended even her sainted recipe so that it can be made easily in this country. The traditional pasta to eat with it are *orecchiette*, or 'little ears', but any small macaroni type pasta that will absorb lots of sauce will do equally well. I suppose it should be called *polpette al ragù*.

Serves 6.

< 219 >

Ingredients

225 g/8 oz onion
2 tins of Italian chopped tomatoes in juice
450 g/1 lb each of minced beef and minced lamb
3 slices of bread turned into fresh breadcrumbs
2 finely chopped cloves of garlic
2 tbsp finely chopped parsley

2 cloves of garlic
½ tsp thyme
½ tsp dried oregano
50 g/2 oz parmesan
6 tbsp olive oil
1 egg

To serve the first course:
450 g/1 lb orecchiette or similar pasta
100 g/4 oz parmesan cheese

To serve the second course:
900 g/2 lb new potatoes
450 g/1 lb green beans, topped, tailed and lightly cooked

Method

Make the tomato sauce by sautéing the finely chopped onion and two cloves of garlic in the olive oil, adding the tins of tomatoes, seasoning generously and simmering. Add the herbs and simmer for 15 minutes. Mix the two meats together with the breadcrumbs, the parsley, cheese, the egg and the finely chopped cloves of garlic. Knead thoroughly with your hands until the mixture becomes firm and coherent. Divide into 12 portions and form oblong patties with these. Fry them gently in a large pan on both sides for about 5 minutes a side until they are well browned. Slide them gently into the tomato sauce and simmer with a lid half on for 45 minutes. If the sauce shows signs of drying out, add a cupful of water and stir gently but do not break up the meat dumplings. Put the pasta on to cook in a pan of boiling salted water for 3–4 minutes. Take off the heat, place on the lid and allow to stand for 7 or 8 minutes. Drain the pasta and stir a little olive oil in and serve with the tomato sauce from the Ragù but without the meat dumplings. This forms the first course.

Serve the dumplings with a little of their tomato sauce still clinging to them, with newly boiled potatoes and the green beans for colour and crunch. A wonderful two course meal with real rustic flavour.

< 220 >

LEMON AND ALMOND TART

This is a perfect tart served warm or cold, when it is wonderfully chewy and sticky. Locally, almonds are used for almost all cooking but it is nice made with walnuts too.

Serves 4–6.

Ingredients

225 g/8 oz ready-made shortcrust pastry, thawed if frozen or 20 cm/8 in shop-bought shortcrust flan case

100 g/4 oz unsalted butter

2 eggs, lightly beaten

225 g/8 oz chopped almonds

175 g/6 oz golden syrup

Grated rind and juice of 1 lemon

Pouring cream, to serve (optional)

Method

Preheat the oven to 350°F/180°C/160°C Fan/Gas Mark 4/bottom of an Aga roasting oven. If using pastry, line a 20 cm/8 in flan tin with it. Either knuckle it in by putting a lump of pastry in the middle of the tin and pressing it down until it fits, or roll it out neatly, press it in and trim off the edges. Prick the pastry all over, put a bit of foil on top, and bake for about 10 minutes. Take it out, leave to cool and then remove the foil. Place the butter, syrup, eggs, lemon juice and rind in a non-stick pan and stir until it has just melted and the syrup is runny enough to blend in with all the rest of the ingredients. Scatter the almonds on to the pastry-lined flan tin or shortcrust flan case and pour in the lemon mixture. Bake for 40–45 minutes until risen and firm to the touch. Serve warm or cold, cut into slices with a little cream if liked.

< 221 >

Cefalu

< **222** >

SICILY

Sicily, the island football that the Italian boot seems always about to kick, was the first of the provinces of ancient Rome and the recently unified Italy. In the intervening period between the fall of the Empire and reunification in the nineteenth century, Sicily was ruled by a range of peoples and empires from one end of Europe to the other – Arabs and Normans, Holy Roman Emperors, Spanish kings, virtually every background and influence except the 'Italian' one.

All over Sicily there are Greek temples and Roman villas in varying states of preservation but indicating the then wealth and richness of the towns and the countryside. Under Arab rule, nearly 1500 years later, the rich soil, deriving from the volcanic attentions of Mount Etna, was developed with a large and complex irrigation system. At the time the climate was wetter and there were rivers flowing in the island. The Arabs tapped this water and planted almond, orange and lemon groves whose descendants today still dominate much of the landscape. Its agriculture has always been at the heart of its wealth although there is some modern industry, much of it based on oil from North Africa, slowly developing. Sicily grows the finest hard (durum) wheat which is the best for making dry or hard pasta and indeed its pasta lunga, spaghetti and long macaroni are the absolute favourites here. Fish dominates the cuisine and although some veal and a little beef is eaten it's rare to find a meal that isn't based on fish. And fish of all kinds. The fishing ports even specialize a little, with Messina in the east famous for its swordfish and Tropanni for its tuna. The whole island is well-known for sardines, and sea bass and even cod are widely enjoyed.

The thing that makes Sicilian cooking most special is the strength of tradition going back to its many masters and rulers, particularly the Saracens, as the Arabs were called by the Sicilians. Not only in the oranges, almonds and lemons eaten in profusion and in savoury and sweet dishes but also with the sweet and sour traditions of street food, often deep fried and full of creamy centres inside a crisp coating. A prime example is the love of aubergines in food of all kinds, in pasta sauces, on their own, in salads, in fish and meat dishes. And last but not least in Sicily's debt to the Arabs are the sweetmeats and desserts. All Sicilian cooking tends towards the flamboyant but the mixtures and exotic combinations that Sicilian pastry chefs and sweet-makers aspire to have distinct Middle Eastern connotations. The world famous Cassatta is not in fact in Sicily an ice-

< 223 >

cream at all but an extraordinary cheesecake made with ewes' milk ricotta and layered with the candied fruit that is famous in the area. The ice-cream version, equally layered and fruited, is a recent development from the availability of artificial freezing techniques of the nineteenth century. This led Sicilian ice-cream makers to travel the world with their skills, especially to America, much of whose own great tradition of ice-cream owes its debt of origin to the streets of Messina and Palermo.

The Sicilians love to entertain, and every opportunity for a party, feast day or wedding, fiesta or event is taken on a grand scale. Caterers abound on the island and special events can often include not only up to thirty or more dishes but also street vendors brought in to cook their specialities as well, for instance hot rice balls stuffed with melted cheese or deep fried octopus. In Sicilian parlance this kind of wonderful extravagance is called *Spagnolismo*, or 'putting on the Spanish style', because in the time of the Spanish aristocracy conspicuous consumption was practised almost as a matter of social necessity. The wonderful Sicilian novel *The Leopard* was written by and tells the story of the last of these great noble families – the Lampedusas, still anxious to live in the way that it had for centuries.

Messina

< 224 >

EATING OUT

Eating out in Sicily can take one of two forms, either the usual one of going to a restaurant or trattoria and eating the local food or, if you're fortunate, to be involved in one of the feasts or spectaculars that so often take place there. If you're staying at one of the big hotels when there is a banquet going on, you can often find yourself involved, voluntarily or involuntarily, in the celebrations. In that case simply look at the spectacle and marvel at it and enjoy yourself. There is no means of pretending moderation at a Sicilian party.

Local cooking however does vary very much from different parts of the island. The western end, Palermo and Trepana, tend to have preserved the Arab traditions rather more strongly than anywhere else, and the use of orange juice, sweet and sour flavours, and some of the more exotic spices, particularly in the sweetmeats, are common. From Trepana round to the south coast there is a surprising connection still with North African dishes. A variety of cous-cous known locally as *cucusu*, a fish soup eaten with the cracked and steamed semolina wheat that is characteristic of North African cooking is a great speciality. On the Greek side of the island, Messina to Syracuse, a more delicate style of cooking is prevalent with a great use of herbs, particularly basil; parsley is used almost as a vegetable, and capers add an unexpected and piquant flavour. Do have pasta with your meal, it is regarded as essential in Sicily, particularly the long, dried pastas with unusual sauces based on sardines or aubergines. A fish dish is essential and will come often with unexpected combinations of flavours from raisins and pine nuts through fennel to chilli. The fresh fruit on the island is wonderful, and the sweetmeats are often kept as a separate course. They tended in the recent past to be made by nuns in convents, who specialized in different shapes and sizes and have some quite extraordinary names, often with a hint of salaciousness about them, such as 'virgin's breasts' or 'nun's thighs'. They are best eaten in quite small quantities as they are extremely rich, sweet and scented.

The most substantial cheese made in Sicily is ricotta and it is used in all kinds of dishes, both savoury and sweet. Indeed it is even sometimes cut in slices and fried. There are some hard cheeses, but none so distinguished as those from the mainland, and probably the best buy for a traveller are some of the wonderful crystallized fruits which almost uniquely, in the Mediterranean, seem to taste more of fruit than of sugar.

Pasta with raw tomato sauce

< 225 >

The fish market – Palermo

< **226** >

PASTA WITH RAW TOMATO SAUCE

Although this version of this dish is attributed to Sicily, in fact pasta with raw tomato sauce exists as far north as Tuscany. The great Sicilian variation is to include toasted almonds in the mixture, which add an unexpected pleasure and crunch. As with so many of these dishes, quantities can vary. This is a tomato-heavy version but the spices and herbs, while important, are a matter of personal balance.

Ingredients

675 g/1½ lb vine ripened dark red tomatoes (no others will do, don't bother if you can't find them)
2 oz blanched toasted almonds (available in supermarkets everywhere)
2 tbsp olive oil
1 clove of garlic
A handful of fresh basil leaves
½ tsp each sugar and chilli powder mixed together
450 g/1 lb spaghetti or its square sectioned equivalent, linguine

Method

Halve the tomatoes and squeeze out any runny pips or juice. Place them with the olive oil, the toasted almonds, the peeled clove of garlic, the basil, the sugar and the chilli in a food processor and rough chop until well blended but not smooth. Allow to stand while you cook the spaghetti. Cook it in plenty of boiling salted water with a drop of oil until just tender. Drain and, while still hot, pour over the sauce and mix thoroughly. Serve immediately. This can be served with or without cheese, but the delicate flavour of the sauce seems not to require it.

PASTA SARDINARA

This extraordinary way of dressing pasta is typically Sicilian. Sometimes sardines – filleted and crisp fried – are added to the dish as it is served, making it much more substantial.

Serves 6 as a starter.

< 227 >

Preparing pasta with raw tomato sauce p. 227

< **228** >

Ingredients

350 g/12 oz rigatoni or any small pasta shape
25 g/1 oz parsley, stalks removed
50 g/2 oz freshly grated parmesan
50 g/2 oz can anchovies in oil, drained

2 slices white bread
1 garlic clove, roughly chopped
120 ml/4 fl oz olive oil
Grated rind of 1 lemon

4 boned crisp fried fresh sardines (optional)

Method

Cook the pasta in a large pan of boiling salted water for 3–4 minutes, then remove from the heat. Cover with a lid and leave to stand for 7 minutes. Drain well. Place the bread in a food processor or liquidizer and turn into breadcrumbs. Add the parsley, parmesan and garlic and process until well combined. Heat the oil in a frying pan and add the anchovies and gently mash together while heating through. Sprinkle with the breadcrumb mixture and add the lemon rind. Turn until lightly browned, then add the pasta and mix together. Serve with extra parmesan, and the sardines if you wish.

BAKED AUBERGINES AND ALMONDS

Aubergines are plentiful in May, it's the beginning of their season in the Mediterranean and we import them from there. On their home turf they're a bread and butter vegetable, part of the basic food of everyday life, but for us they're still a little more exotic than their regular colleagues, courgettes and peppers. The addition of almonds is the Sicilian touch.

Serves 4.

Ingredients

2 x 225–300 g/8–10 oz aubergines
1 garlic clove, crushed
Juice of half a lemon

75 ml/3 fl oz olive oil
25 g/1 oz chopped fresh parsley
75 g/3 oz slivered almonds

Crusty bread, to serve

< 229 >

Method

Preheat the oven to 350°F/180°C/170°C Fan/Gas Mark 4/bottom of an Aga roasting oven. Split the aubergines in half and arrange in an oiled baking dish. Bake for 45 minutes until the aubergines are soft. Leave to cool a little. Very carefully spoon out the centre of each aubergine half, leaving the shells, and mix the flesh with the garlic, two tablespoons of the olive oil, the parsley and lemon juice. Pile the mixture back in the shells and top with the slivered almonds. Sprinkle the remaining olive oil on top and return to the oven for 10 minutes until the almonds are just crisping. Serve at once with plenty of bread.

INSALATA DI TONNO

Surprisingly, on this island of fresh fish, this dish is made with tinned tuna, though connoisseurs of the varieties look for tins marked 'ventresca' which are supposed to contain the most delicate and well flavoured part of the tuna. Although we tend to buy it in little tins, tuna often comes in Italy from the delicatessen counter, where the tins run to kilos rather than ounces. Either way, this combination of vegetables, eggs and fish makes a pleasant Italian use of the ingredients which further north would be thought of as the basis of a Salad Niçoise.

Ingredients

225 g/8 oz tinned tuna, drained from its oil

450 g/1 lb new potatoes	2 eggs
1 small tin anchovy fillets	12 black olives
2 gherkins	1 tbsp capers (optional)
2 tbsp white wine vinegar	2 tbsp olive oil
Juice of half a lemon	Black pepper

Method

Scrub and boil the potatoes until they are just cooked. Allow them to cool a little, split them in half and sprinkle with the juice of the lemon. Break up the tuna into

< 230 >

Cod with tomatoes & sweet peppers p. 232; sea bass with fennel p. 233 insalata di tonno p. 230;

< **231** >

chunks and mix with the potatoes. Hard boil the eggs (this can be done at the same time as cooking the potatoes) for 8–10 minutes. Put them into cold water, shell and cut into quarters. Rough chop the gherkins and the capers and the anchovy fillets together. Mix the vinegar and the olive oil with the anchovy mixture and pour over the potatoes, eggs and tuna. Decorate with the black olives and grind plenty of black pepper over the top before serving. It shouldn't need any more salt. It can sit happily in the fridge for up to an hour.

COD WITH TOMATOES AND SWEET PEPPERS

The combination of colours and flavours in this dish is stunning. It can be made with any white fish like coley or hake but cod steaks are perfect for it with their meaty texture and snow-white appearance when cooked.

Serves 4.

Ingredients

225 g/8 oz onion, thinly sliced

1 each small red and yellow pepper, seeded and sliced

400 g/14 oz can chopped tomatoes

1 tbsp chopped fresh thyme or 1 tsp dried

Chopped fresh parsley, to garnish

4 tbsp olive oil

½ tsp dried chilli flakes

Juice of 1 small lemon

4 x 175 g/6 oz cod steaks

New potatoes, to serve

Method

Heat the oil in a large frying pan, add the onions and cook gently for 3–4 minutes until softened but not browned. Add the peppers and cook for another 2–3 minutes. Add the tomatoes, thyme, chilli flakes and lemon juice, bring to the boil, season generously and simmer for about 5 minutes, stirring occasionally until the mixture has thickened slightly. Place the cod steaks on top of the tomato mixture, cover the pan tightly and simmer for about 10–12 minutes until the fish is steamed through. You will be able to tell this because it will have taken on a marvellous snow-white opacity. Garnish with parsley and serve with the potatoes.

< 232 >

SEA BASS WITH FENNEL

Anywhere it's caught, sea bass is regarded as a speciality and that's just as much the case in Sicily as elsewhere. This dish is also made with bream and with large red mullet, both of which have a stronger flavour but are equally successful in their way. This is a dish for special occasions, both in terms of its ingredients and in the spectacular presentation it makes. When you serve it, make sure that each person gets a portion of fish and vegetables. Other ingredients are best left to other courses.

Ingredients

2 x 450 g/1 lb sea bass or bream, scaled, cleaned and rinsed

450 g/1 lb fennel

6 tbsp olive oil

Juice of 1 lemon

1 clove of garlic

Method

Trim the fennel and slice it lengthways into 5 mm/¼ in slices. Put the oil into a large pan and stir-fry the fennel gently for about 10–15 minutes. If it starts to look too brown, add a tablespoon of water to prevent the vegetable browning. As the fennel starts to turn gold, push it to the side of the pan and add the fish. Season them and the fennel generously and turn once to coat with the oil. Cover and cook for about 7 minutes a side until the fish is cooked through but not in any way dry. Remove the fish to a warm serving dish. Turn the fennel in the oil so that it absorbs all the flavours and serve alongside the fish. It's probably best to fillet this as you serve it. Half a side of fish to a person. Just before eating, squeeze the lemon juice over the fish and fennel and season.

< 233 >

PESCESPADA A GHIOTTA

This way of cooking swordfish, a famous Sicilian dish, involves almost all the flavourings that seem to typify the island's cookery. Swordfish is surprisingly widely available in Britain these days, but if it's not around when you are looking for it, it is possible to make this dish with tuna steaks, although obviously the flavour comes out differently. Either way, the steaks should be about 150–225 g/6–8 oz each and about 1 cm/½ in thick. This is a rich and powerfully flavoured dish, not for the faint-hearted or those unsure if they like fish. For enthusiasts it can be quite an extraordinary treat. It certainly needs nothing with it except plenty of good crusty bread, and a salad to follow.

Ingredients

4 plum or vine ripened tomatoes (or half a tin of Italian chopped tomato)
4 swordfish steaks, 150–225 g/6–8 oz   100 ml/4 fl oz olive oil
1 medium onion   1 clove of garlic
1 tin anchovy fillets in oil   2 stalks of celery
12 stoneless green olives (not stuffed with pimento)   ½ tsp dried rosemary
1 tbsp each of capers and parsley   225 g/8 oz new potatoes

Method

Trim the swordfish steaks. Heat the oil in a large frying pan into which they will all go at the same time, and fry them gently for 4 minutes a side. While the fish is frying, scrub the potatoes and put them to boil until they are barely tender, about 8–10 minutes. Take them out, drain them and halve them. Remove the fish from the oil, and keep warm with the potatoes. Peel and finely chop the garlic, onion and celery and add that, with the tin of anchovies and its oil, the parsley, rosemary and chopped tomatoes, to the fish pan. Stir the mixture together and simmer for 15 minutes until well blended. Rough chop the capers and olives and add those to the sauce. Season generously with pepper and test for salt (the anchovies contain a lot). Add the fish to the sauce, spooning it over it carefully, and stir the potatoes in at the sides. As soon as the fish and potatoes are up to full heat again, serve immediately sprinkled with a little extra parsley.

< 234 >

COTOLETTE ALLA PALERMITANA

As Marcella Hazan remarks in her Second Classic Italian Cookbook, 'Anywhere in the world but Palermo a breaded veal cutlet is fried. There it is grilled, and a marvellous difference it makes.' In fact, grilling breadcrumbed cutlets is not unique to Palermo as the French have been doing it for quite a while, but she's right about it being marvellous. Usually Palermians mix breadcrumbs and finely chopped rosemary in the coating, but I prefer it without as much rosemary as is traditional in that city. These days, although veal reared in humane conditions is widely available, some people have developed a resistance to it and you might want to try this dish with thinly beaten turkey escalopes, which provide a similar texture if not quite the same flavour. Either way, the meat needs to be beaten quite thin, which is best achieved between two sheets of wetted greaseproof paper, using a heavy frying pan as the hammer.

Ingredients

675 g/1½ lb veal or turkey escalopes
4 tbsp olive oil
Juice of 1 lemon
½ tsp salt
½ tsp finely chopped rosemary leaves
225 g/8 oz fresh white breadcrumbs, toasted in the oven until dry but not coloured

Method

Make sure the meat is flattened into sheets not more than 1 cm/½ in thick. Pour over the lemon juice and allow to marinate for at least 10 minutes and up to 6 hours before using. When ready to cook, preheat the grill for at least 10 minutes. This will not work with a barbecue. Mix the salt and the finely chopped rosemary with the breadcrumbs. Take the meat from the lemon juice marinade and dry it lightly on kitchen paper. Rub all over with the olive oil and dip onto the breadcrumb plate, making sure that each side is as evenly coated as possible. When all the veal has been coated, place it on the rack of the grill, which has been lightly brushed with olive oil, and grill for about 2–2½ minutes a side, allowing the breadcrumbs to take colour but not to blacken. Turn carefully and serve as soon as both sides are cooked. A little flavoured olive oil, rosemary or herbs or lemon, is often dribbled over the cutlets before they're eaten. Young broad beans or a mixture of broad beans and artichoke hearts and sautéd potatoes are a wonderful accompaniment.

< 235 >

PEACH ICE-CREAM

Ice-creams in Sicily come in all shapes and sizes, in tall glasses and in flat dishes, in cones and in complex confections. My favourites depend on mood, place and time but a perennial choice is peach ice-cream. Properly made it has bits of peach in it and a unique flavour. This method is designed to work without a home ice-cream maker, and leaves you with a smooth ice-cream and slightly chewy frozen bits of fruit.

Ingredients

125 ml/5 fl oz double cream
4 separated eggs
4 tbsp icing sugar
1 tsp vanilla essence
225 g/8 oz peeled, stoned, fresh peaches
2 tbsp caster sugar
4 tbsp water

Method

Slice the peaches 1 cm/½ in thick. Melt the caster sugar in the water and poach gently for about 10 minutes until the peach slices are translucent. Meanwhile, whisk the cream until it's really thick. Take two of the egg whites and whisk them until they're thick and add them to the cream. Beat the four yolks thoroughly together and whisk in the icing sugar tablespoon by tablespoon until it's thoroughly incorporated and the whole mixture is pale and frothy. Add the vanilla essence and whisk gently again. Purée half the peach slices and mix them into the ice-cream mixture. Rough chop the remainder and add those. Mix thoroughly together, put into a plastic container and place in a freezer for about 4–5 hours until frozen solid. If you have an ice-cream maker you could make the ice-cream much more quickly in that following its instructions. You do not need to take this mixture out to beat it or process it while it's freezing. Before you eat it, leave it in the fridge for half an hour to soften slightly. It is particularly nice with thin almond biscuits.

< 236 >

Sicilian cheesecake p. 238; peach ice-cream p. 236

< 237 >

SICILIAN CHEESECAKE

In its native Sicily this is the dish that is known as Cassata, not an ice-cream confection but a rather fancy cheesecake. In this crafty version I've made it as simple as possible without losing any of the delicious flavours. You will need to find ricotta, the Italian equivalent of cottage cheese as this is a recipe where cottage cheese will not substitute. Supermarkets and delicatessen counters all sell it these days anyway.

Serves 4.

Ingredients

1 x 20 cm/8 in sponge cake, homemade or shop-bought
6 tbsp freshly squeezed orange juice
100 g/4 oz caster sugar
350 g/12 oz fresh ricotta cheese
Pinch of ground cinnamon
225 g/8 oz crystallized fruit (or chopped mixed peel if all else fails)
50 g/2 oz bitter chocolate, chopped into slivers
Icing sugar, to decorate

Method

Split the sponge cake horizontally into two. Place the bottom half on a serving plate and sprinkle with four tablespoons of the orange juice. Put the caster sugar into a pan with two tablespoons of water, bring to the boil and beat into the ricotta with the cinnamon. Mix till completely smooth. Rough chop the crystallized fruit leaving one or two of the cherries in quite large pieces. Mix 175 g/6 oz of that into the ricotta with half of the chocolate. Spread the filling over the bottom half of the sponge cake, add the top half of the sponge cake and sprinkle that in turn with the remaining orange juice. Press down gently to make sure it's firm without squeezing all the filling out. Decorate with the icing sugar and the reserved crystallized fruit and chocolate. Chill for at least 1 hour and up to two days. Serve straight from the fridge and cut like a cake.

< 238 >

INDEX

< 239 >

< 240 >